WINNING THE JURY'S ATTENTION

Presevidence
from V
o Closing

Trey Cox

AMERICAN BAR ASSOCIATION
Section of Litigation

FIRST
CHAIR
·PRESS·

Cover design by Bobbie Sanchez/ABA Publishing.

Printed in the United States of America

15 14 13 12 11   5 4 3 2

Library of Congress Cataloging-in-Publication Data

Cox, Trey.
   Winning the jury's attention / by Trey Cox.—1st ed.
      p. cm.
   Includes bibliographical references and index.
   ISBN 978-1-61632-068-3 (alk. paper)
   1. Jury—United States. I. Title.
   KF8972.C69 2011
   347.73'752--dc23

2011024574

Discounts are available for books ordered in bulk. Special consideration is given to state bars, CLE programs, and other bar-related organizations. Inquire at Book Publishing, ABA Publishing, American Bar Association, 321 N. Clark Street, Chicago, Illinois 60654-7598.

www.ababooks.org

CONTENTS

Acknowledgments   vii

About the Author   ix

Chapter 1

Meet the "Modern Juror"   1

    1. Hey, Look at Me!   3

    2. Introducing the Seven Principles   4

Chapter 2

Taking the Voodoo out of Voir Dire   7

    1. Getting Things Started   11

    2. Challenging Jurors for Cause   24

Chapter 3

The Science of the Brain as It Relates to Trial Presentations   27

Chapter 4

A Closer Look at the Seven Principles   35

    1. The Personal Credibility Principle: *Demonstrate competence, accuracy, leadership, and efficiency to gain credibility.*   *35*

    2. *The Road Map Principle: People learn better when the material is presented with clear outlines and headings.*   *36*

    3. *The Chunking Principle: People learn better when information is presented in bite-sized chunks.*   *37*

    4. *The Multimedia Principle: People learn better from words and pictures than from words alone.*   *38*

5. *The "Less Is More" Principle: People learn better
   when extraneous material is excluded.*   *39*

6. *The Stickiness Principle: Make your themes and ideas "sticky."*   *40*

7. *The Jolt Principle: Periodically jolt your jury so they do not bolt.*   *41*

Chapter 5

**The Personal Credibility Principle: Demonstrate
Competence, Integrity, and Efficiency to Gain Credibility**   **45**

1. The Credibility Gap   45

2. Building Credibility and Using It in the Courtroom   47

3. Learning from the Master: Aristotle   49

4. Ethos: Credibility Through Appearance   50

Chapter 6

What Trial Lawyers Learn from Actors   **59**

1. Remain Cool, Calm, and Confident   62

2. Pathos: Building Empathy   66

Chapter 7

Maintaining Credibility Through Cross-Examination   **73**

The Three Techniques of Cross-Examination   73

Chapter 8

The Signaling Principle: What's Next and Are We There Yet?   **97**

1. The Opening Statement: Transitions and Signposts   98

2. Logos: Developing Your Presentation   99

3. Organizing Your Presentation   104

Chapter 9

**The Segmentation Principle: People Learn Better When
Information Is Presented in Bite-Sized Segments**   **113**

1. The Rule of Three   113

2. What's Your Headline?   117

3. Preparing the Wrap-up   122

Chapter 10

**The Multimedia Principle: People Learn Better from Words
and Pictures than from Words Alone**   **125**

1. Less Is More   126
2. Polish Your Text   130
3. The Power of Props   131
4. Boardwork   132
5. Flip Charts   133
6. Overheads   134

Chapter 11

**The Coherence Less-Is-More Principle: People Learn Better
When Extraneous Material Is Excluded**   **137**

1. Curse of Knowledge   138
2. Keeping It Simple   141

Chapter 12

Stickiness Principle: How to Make an Idea Stick   **145**

1. The Jitters   146
2. Achieving SUCCESs   148

Chapter 13

**The Jolt Principle: Periodically Jolt Your Jury
so They Do Not Bolt**   **159**

1. Grab Them at the Start   160
2. Move It!   162

Chapter 14

Arming Your Jurors for the "Final Argument"   **165**

1. What Is the Purpose of the Closing Statement?   166
2. Persuading the Jury: Closing Statement + Summation =
   Final Argument   167
3. Structuring the Argument   170
4. Nuts and Bolts of a Closing Statement   173

5. Burden of Proof   178
6. Circumstantial Evidence   180
7. Ethics and Objections   180
8. Delivering the Summation   182
9. Conclusion   183

Index   **185**

Acknowledgments

I would like to thank my wife, Erin, and my daughters Amelia, Cate, and Vivian, for their support during the many nights and weekends I spent writing and editing. I would like to thank my Mom who taught me the value of teaching and my Dad who inspired me to be a lawyer. I would also like to thank John Evans, who taught me to write; my partners Mike, Jeff, and Eric, who taught me everything I know about the courtroom; and Sarah Forbes Orwig, my editor, who kept me between the yellow lines and moving forward on this project. I am blessed with many great and supportive people in my life. This book would not have happened without them all.

About the Author

Trey Cox specializes in high-stakes business disputes. His jury trial experience and courtroom success have earned him the distinction of being Board Certified as a Trial Advocate by the National Board of Trial Advocacy. Mr. Cox is based in Dallas, Texas and represents Fortune 500 corporations, entrepreneurs and leading firms across the country in a wide array of industries. His dedication to his clients and winning track record have repeatedly earned him local, state and national recognition as a top trial lawyer:

> Honored as a "Leader in His Field" in Chambers & Partners 2009-2011 USA Guide to Leading Lawyers—General Commercial Litigation (Texas)
> Listed with Best Lawyers® in America, 2009-2011
> Listed as a "Texas Super Lawyer" by *Law & Politics*, 2004–2011
> Selected by *The Dallas Business Journal* as a "Defender" in 2008 and "One of the 10 Metroplex Litigators Worth Having on Your Side."
> Recognized by his peers in *D Magazine* as a "Best Lawyer Under 40" for five consecutive years
> AV rated by Martindale Hubbell
> Named one of the "Best and Brightest Business Leaders" in *The Dallas Business Journal's* "40 Under 40" survey

Progressive and innovative, Mr. Cox has earned a reputation as a pioneer in combining technology and neuroscientific principles to improve jury communication and persuasion. He graduated magna cum laude from Washington and Lee University and was named the Wilkinson Scholar; is a member of Phi Beta Kappa as well as Omicron Delta Kappa; and was awarded the Algernon Sydney Sullivan Award by the faculty. In 1995, he received his law degree from the University of Virginia, where he served as the Executive Editor of the Journal of Law & Politics. After serving as a law clerk to the Honorable Jacques L. Wiener, Jr., of the United States Court of Appeals for the Fifth Circuit, Mr. Cox joined what is now Lynn

Tillotson Pinker & Cox, LLP, in 1997. He serves on the faculty of Southern Methodist University Law School and the National Institute for Trial Advocacy. He has lectured throughout the country, and authored numerous legal articles, white papers, and books. He is married to Erin Nealy Cox, the head of the Dallas office of digital forensic firm Stroz Friedberg's, and is the father of three daughters, Amelia, Cate, and Vivian.

CHAPTER 1

Meet the "Modern Juror"

"A wealth of information creates a poverty of attention."
—*Herbert Simon, Nobel Prize-winning economist*

Juror 12 is adrift. It's not that he doesn't care about your contract dispute. Who knows, he *might* even be the kind of natural leader who can rally 11 wafflers to your side during deliberations. The real problem with Juror 12 is his irrepressible urge to manage his bloated e-mail folder with his cell phone keypad, and his desire to cram as much business as possible into each recess. If you compete for Juror 12's attention by droning on, cramming PowerPoint slides with endless bullets, clumsily admitting exhibits, and using arcane techniques or convoluted questions to elicit witness testimony, you'll be lucky if he hears, much less recalls, any of the facts or arguments you put before him.

Meet today's juror, so overloaded with information that he can barely focus on the important things in his own life, much less those in your case. Chances are, more than half the jurors on your panel belong to my generation, Generation X—or even more challenging, Generation Y—raised with a TV in every room, smart phones in their pockets, and iPods at their ears. Research shows that people today process more information in a 24-hour period than the average person 500 years ago would have come across in a lifetime.

Unfortunately, connecting and engaging these days aren't simply generational problems; they're a struggle for all of us. Nor are these challenges limited to the courtroom. This pervasive attention-deficit phenomenon has been widely documented, most notably in the influential and provocative Harvard Business Press book, *The Attention Economy*,[1] which explains how the barrage of information in our daily lives exceeds our own individual attention bandwidth. Understanding this crisis has

---

1. Thomas H. Davenport & John C. Beck, The Attention Economy: Understanding the New Currency of Business (2001).

real-world value for business leaders who increasingly struggle with information-flooded employees, clients, and customers while parceling out their own attention in the face of a relentless multimedia barrage of information.

> Telecommunications bandwidth is not a problem, but human bandwidth is. At one point, software magnates had the ambition to put "information at your fingertips." Now we've got it, and in vast quantities. But no one will be informed by it, learn from it, or act on it unless they've got some free attention to devote to the information.[2]

We've all seen (and, to be honest with ourselves, we've all displayed) the symptoms of distraction: careless mistakes, disorganization, and forgetfulness, as well as problems sustaining attention and following instructions, and losing things. If you've tried a case in the last 12 months, I'd bet that you witnessed jurors exhibiting ADD-like symptoms: Juror 3 is staring into space; Juror 9 is sneaking a peek at his "CrackBerry"; and Juror 6 is like my three-year-old in Sunday Mass—she couldn't sit still even if I Super-Glued her to the seat. Sadly, I'm not making this stuff up. It's gotten so bad that the *New York Times* wrote about jurors "tweeting" about their experiences . . . during trials![3] In a case in Arkansas, tweeting was the basis for a request for mistrial in which a construction company lost a $12.6 million suit. Although the alleged offender's attorney denies that any of the tweets were made before the jury's decision, tweets such as "'So, Jonathan, what did you do today?' Oh, nothing really. I just gave away TWELVE MILLION DOLLARS of somebody else's money!" and "Oh, and nobody buy Stoam. It's bad mojo, and they'll probably cease to exist, now that their wallet is $12M lighter. http://www.stoam.com/"[4] could destroy weeks of testimony and evidence and put the case back at square one.

Accordingly, jurors suffering from distracted attention and technology addiction can be frustrating because their education and employment backgrounds in occupations as postal workers, data entry technicians, computer programmers, and even doctors lead you to believe they would be good jurors for your complicated case. But in the thick of trial testimony, these same capable, accomplished, and intelligent individuals daydream or fidget compulsively, unable to focus long enough for you to

---

2. *Id.* at 2–3.
3. John Schwartz, *As Jurors Turn to Web, Mistrials Are Popping Up,* N.Y. Times, Mar. 18, 2009, at A1.
4. http://arstechnica.com/web/news/2009/03/jurors-twitter-posts-cited-in-motion-for-mistrial.ars.

communicate the themes, ideas, and connections that will demonstrate why your client should prevail. Plus, the products of their distraction—wiggling in the chair or tapping their pencils—can disrupt the entire panel, further frustrating your ability to communicate with the jury. Also, technology and their need for constant communication and updates can potentially damage your case, as in the Arkansas disaster.

Think about complex litigation and imagine the challenge of introducing technical concepts like the distressed securities market or the nuances of a double-bypass surgery on a 57-year-old diabetic patient. These types of explanations can be long and boring—easily drifting into a real yawn-fest. And keeping the jury's attention while you give them the background is not your only job. After you've educated them on the complexities of your case, you must then persuade them that your client's actions were warranted and appropriate for the given circumstances in order to garner a favorable decision.

So, what do we do? We must adapt. We have to find a better way to communicate and lead jurors through the factual forest of a trial. Rather than wring our hands and lament the difficulties we face as trial lawyers (all the while, using the same tired trial presentation techniques), we must explore new methods. The fields of marketing, education, and broadcast news can teach us a lot about how to adapt our presentation methods, and ensure that we present a compelling story that maintains the attention of even the most distracted and distractible jurors.

I maintain there's nothing wrong with the jury trial system as a means to resolve factual disputes. Jurors get it right most of the time, often despite the lawyering rather than because of it. The problem lies with the presentation techniques that trial lawyers utilize to present their cases to juries. In *The Attention Economy*, Davenport and Beck teach business leaders to treat their employees' attention as a scarce resource. We must do the same in the courtroom. We must realize that a juror's attention is a precious commodity and should never be wasted. As trial lawyers, we must find the best way to get and keep their attention in order to communicate our core ideas.

1. Hey, Look at Me!

The first hurdle in the clear communication race is getting people's attention. The juror's attention is the one thing that any trial lawyer must have if he wants to communicate his message and win his case. But let's face it. Today's jurors, consumed in their own demanding personal and professional lives, are not going to just hand over their undivided attention for as long as you want to stand in front of them and talk. In the courtroom, you cannot *demand* attention, you must *attract* attention. To do this, you must do a very, very good job of choosing the right message, presenting it in the right way, and doing so in the right amount of time.

These days, no one but scholars and fanatics are willing to soldier through hour after hour of explanation about anything. Our ability to pay attention no longer includes sitting through lengthy and tedious presentations. Today, a two-hour movie is the high-water mark for how long anyone will sit in one place, and movies are carefully orchestrated visual feasts populated with beautiful, interesting people. Plus, movies are designed solely to entertain.

Consider the CLE seminars we're required to sit through each year. No presentation lasts more than 50 minutes. More often, each segment is divided into 30-minute sessions, often supported by entertaining visuals and interactive participation. Even so, we struggle to focus on the message. Most of us can't resist checking our e-mail. If you can't bring yourself to focus on a presentation in your chosen profession, how do you think it feels to be a juror in a case about which you know little and care less?

2. Introducing the Seven Principles

So how do you reach a juror who can't or won't settle down and listen? In this book, I present seven principles for communicating effectively with your jury. Implementing the practical techniques through each phrase of trial will help you connect with the jury, direct and hold their attention where you want it, and promote understanding and memory.

1. *The Personal Credibility Principle:* Demonstrate competence, accuracy, leadership, and efficiency to gain credibility.
2. *The Signaling Principle:* People learn better when the material is presented with clear outlines and headings.
3. *The Segmentation Principle:* People learn better when information is presented in bite-sized chunks.

4. *The Multimedia Principle:* People learn better from words and pictures than from words alone.
5. *The Coherence Principle:* People learn better when extraneous material is excluded.
6. *The Stickiness Principle:* Make your themes and ideas "sticky."
7. *The Jolt Principle:* Periodically jolt your jury so they don't bolt.

The principles will be explored in depth in Chapter 4. In Chapters 5 through 13 are courtroom-tested techniques that you can use to prepare for trial *right now*.

In this book, we'll talk about the science of the brain and the proven psychological theories that underlie my principles. I am not a neuroscientist. I am a courtroom lawyer. I help clients explain why they are right. Over the course of trying cases the last 15 years I have discovered, somewhat by accident, that learning more about how people think, receive, and retain information made a big difference in how juries heard and perceived me. When I could not find a book that explained my most useful discoveries about the brain in simple language that could be applied to the courtroom, I decided to write one. We'll touch on the modern science of psychology, cognitive psychology, and cognitive neuroscience. Fundamentally, this is a book of practical advice that will help you make and deliver an effective trial presentation step-by-step.

Imitation is the sincerest form of flattery. Few of the ideas presented are original to me. I have shamelessly begged, borrowed, and stolen from many great thinkers and sources, including *Beyond Bullet Points* by Cliff Atkinson,[5] *Presentation Zen* by Garr Reynolds,[6] and *Made to Stick: Why Some Ideas Survive and Others Die* by Chip and Dan Heath.[7]

I won't tie you down with rules that will make your trial presentation formulaic, dry, or lacking in personal style. My intent is the exact opposite. Your creativity will have plenty of leeway. At the same time, if you design your presentation according to the recommendations offered here, you will play to the strengths of those who see and hear it, and will avoid being defeated, that is, misunderstood or ignored, because of the inherent weakness of human mental processes.

---

5. Cliff Atkinson, Beyond Bullet Points (2005).
6. Garr Reynolds, Presentation Zen (2008).
7. Dan Heath & Chip Heath, Made to Stick: Why Some Ideas Survive and Others Die (2d ed. 2008).

We should use trial presentations not to dazzle the courtroom, but to communicate the meat of our ideas. Communication is only effective when the audience receives and understands the message. Otherwise, words just wash over them. In this book I provide clear instructions that you can follow to make your ideas crystal-clear and immediately comprehensible. I also go deeper than that. I will help you develop intuitions about how to present your ideas and themes at trial.

Reading the chapters in order will alter your view of juries and open your eyes to a creative and innovative way of crafting and delivering your trial presentations. You can then revisit the specific techniques outlined in each chapter as you prepare for your next encounter with the "modern juror." In the next chapter, we'll take the voodoo out of voir dire.

CHAPTER 2

Taking the Voodoo out of Voir Dire

> **"A jury consists of 12 persons chosen to decide
> who has the better lawyer."**
> —*Robert Frost*

There is nothing mystical about voir dire. People come with their preprogrammed biases, and there is no black magic that will change that. Voir dire is necessarily a commonsense endeavor. You should have three very specific goals in mind and you should conduct voir dire in a way that best meets those goals.

Since you can't change people's minds, your first goal in voir dire should be to root out their biases in order to lay the foundation for causal challenges. The last thing any lawyer wants is to debrief a jury after losing a case and discover that the outcome could have been different but for an errant juror or two who slipped through the cracks during voir dire. Thus, much of this chapter will be dedicated to asking precise questions that will force potentially adverse jurors to commit to a position that is prejudicial to your client.

The second goal of voir dire is getting the potential jurors to trust you and sympathize with your client. The most effective way of doing this is to have an open and honest dialogue with the venire. If jurors think that you are hiding something from them, they will be skeptical of your case throughout the trial. Voir dire is your chance to build credibility, which has the added benefit of making potential jurors more willing to speak openly about their biases. And the more bias you can eliminate, the better your client's chance of a winning trial. As such, this chapter will also focus not simply on getting the jurors to like you, but also on getting them to trust you.

The final goal is to seek out favorable jurors and to shield them from strikes. It's no secret that winning or losing a case at trial may depend almost entirely on the jurors chosen to hear the case. When assessing juror qualifications, the court looks for the ability to be impartial, whereas lawyers look for "ringers" who will win or lose the case for them during deliberation. To that end, this chapter will emphasize techniques that will help you spot those in the venire that will be your best advocates in the jury room.

Of course, while you are trying to accomplish these goals to advance your client's interests, your opponent is doing the same. Every attorney would like to empanel a jury that is sympathetic to their side and hostile to their opponent's. But the broader interests of justice depend on an adversarial system in which opposing sides seek to further competing interests. A balance is struck when both sides fight vigorously to empanel a favorable jury. That is to say, you too must fight vigorously, or face the consequences of fighting an uphill battle throughout the trial.

But there is a caveat to this—the ability to influence jury selection is limited in a number of jurisdictions. In many federal courts, the presiding judge will pose all or a substantial amount of the voir dire examination, and counsel has only a very limited number of peremptory strikes. In state courts, however, lawyers are generally given more information and wider latitude in the juror selection process. Before conducting voir dire, you should familiarize yourself with the court's rules and practices regarding jury selection and prepare meticulously for this critical process.

Also keep in mind that while you're picking your favorite jurors, every member of the venire is picking their favorite lawyer. Some of them will look for clues about the case, while others will focus on your credibility and competence. But no matter what they're concentrating on, all of them will be forming impressions of you that will last until the final words of your summation. So to meet your goals of eliminating biased jurors, getting the venire to sympathize with your client, and finding your advocates for the jury room, you must develop a good rapport with the venire.

This is no easy task, given that many of them will have never done this before. And admitting one's biases to a lawyer in a courtroom full of strangers is not the most pleasant experience. So you must take steps to reduce the tension and anxiety everyone feels. Here are some great suggestions for doing this from Robert A. Clifford:[1]

---

1. *Adapted from* Robert A. Clifford, *Deselecting the Jury in a Civil Case*, 30 Lᴛɪɢ. J. 8, 12–13 (2004).

> *You only get one chance to make a first impression*. From the moment you set foot in the courtroom, the venire panel is watching your every move. Indeed, they have little else to look at, and you're where the action is. You must be a leader in the courtroom. You must also be up-front and honest. When describing your case, don't hide the bad facts. Instead, take them head-on and admit a problem or weakness, but explain why those facts should not affect the jury's decision in the case.

> *Value the jury's time*. By now, the jurors have experienced firsthand how inefficient the legal process can be. Explain to them that the process can be slow at times, but that deliberate pace is necessary to ensure that justice is served. Also, thank the venire panel for taking time out of their busy schedules to be a part of the process. This is your opportunity to show them that you, perhaps unlike your opponent, will be concise and efficient throughout the trial. The jury will appreciate the fact that you value their time, and this will work in your favor.

> *Address jurors individually*. If you use the jurors' names, you should maintain the appropriate level of formality for the courtroom by addressing them as Mr. or Ms., not by their first names. If you can't use their names, then use their juror numbers so you will have a clear record for appeal.

> *Avoid monotony*. Do not ask questions row by row, juror by juror. This will be boring for some jurors, and most jurors will prepare their answers ahead of time. You're looking for honesty, and that goal is undermined when jurors have prepared their answers. So vary your questions with each juror. When you get a good answer, ask the group if they agree with it. Hone in on those people who disagree. This will help move things along more quickly and give your voir dire a more conversational tone.

> *Be polite and respectful*. Get in the habit of saying "please" and "thank you." Not using these niceties will be more likely to offend someone than using them. Also, acknowledge that some answers may be embarrassing or very personal. Apologize in advance for these, and let the jury know that you're not just asking them to prod into their personal lives, but rather to make sure that you are selecting the best people for the job.

> *Don't be cute. Be human.* A little humility goes a long way. As the old saying goes, "Don't say it. Show it." A juror's perception based on your actions goes much further than your own self-congratulatory

remarks. If you try to ingratiate yourself with potential jurors, you run the risk that they will see through the act. And even if you convince them that you're the best lawyer in the world, rest assured that they will assign extra significance to any mistakes you make at trial. Also, stay away from personal exploits. The jurors don't care about your war stories. Instead, focus on building credibility with the jurors.

> *Don't speak like a lawyer.* We're told from day one of law school that lawyers speak another language than everyone else—"legalese." But many lawyers seem to forget how abrasive it sounds to nonlawyers. Even the most educated jurors will not have the legal background to understand the significance of words like "consideration" and "malfeasance." And phrases like "heretofore" and "to the extent that" tend to make you look pompous. Speak in plain language, as though you're addressing a respected nonlawyer family member. In my trial advocacy class at Southern Methodist University Law School, I bring my fourth-grade daughter to participate in the voir dire exercise to emphasize this point. This is not to say that all jurors have the equivalent of a fourth-grade education, but it emphasizes to my students that they should keep their language clean and simple. Never talk down to the jurors or patronize them. Avoid pretension and pomposity. Nothing turns a juror off faster than a self-righteous, arrogant attorney, and there have been cases in which jurors make decisions not based on evidence but on how much they like or dislike the attorneys. This is evidenced in many cases. One recent example occurred in *Oklahoma v. Raye Dawn Smith.*[2] In an affidavit by a former colleague of a juror, the witness stated,

> [The juror] told me that she had sat on two other juries previous to this case and that during her previous jury service she would sit there bored out of her head looking for anything to distract herself. [The juror] also advised that with her previous jury service she would know how she was going to vote before hearing any of the evidence by selecting a side based on which attorney she liked best. She advised that she was not concerned with the facts, but was more interested in how the attorneys presented the case to the jury.

Ethical? No! Common? Yes!

---

2. Oklahoma v. Smith, No. CF-20070134 (Dist. Ct. Creek County 2007).

> *Be confident*. The jurors will observe your interaction with others in the courtroom. They should notice your rapport with the clerk, bailiff, and the other court personnel.

See Chapter 5 for more information on building credibility with the jury.

1. Getting Things Started

Since every trial is different, I suggest that you evaluate whether a jury consultant can assist in identifying favorable jurors or disqualifying potentially harmful jurors based on factors such as education and economics. The expense associated with jury consultants may not be practical in garden-variety cases but could make sense in very large cases. An alternative to using professional jury consultants is to enlist the help of an experienced local trial lawyer who has tried cases in the locality of the trial. If a jury consultant is out of the question, allow me to share some guidance from my experience in dealing with the voir dire process.

Begin with introductions. Before asking any questions, introduce yourself, your client, and your team. The jury is watching you and wants to be informed. Who are you? Who is your team? The manner in which you introduce your colleagues says a lot about you and how you treat people. By introducing each member of your team, you demonstrate to the jury that you value their contribution. To the jury, ask open-ended questions ("Please tell me about . . .") that prompt jurors to tell you who they really are, what they feel, and what their experiences have been. Make it your aim to establish a trusting relationship.

People tend to be more willing to reciprocate if you have already opened up and trusted them. After you introduce yourself, your team (when applicable), and your client, share something more personal about yourself. Following your opening words, share a short, personal anecdote and connect it with the voir dire process. I often explain that I love football, especially LSU football. Both of my parents graduated from LSU. My dad went to law school at LSU. My father-in-law played on the 1958 LSU national championship team. And my mother-in-law was an LSU Golden Girl. I have attended nearly every LSU home game since I was two years old. I then add that even though I am a lawyer and know every rule in football, I would not be the best referee for an LSU game. It would be impossible for me to be fair, because I love LSU. And I confess that I have never seen an LSU player hold or commit pass interference. I then tie that to the voir dire process by saying that I am trying to identify anyone who would not be the best juror for this particular case, just as I could never referee an LSU football game because of past experiences or opinions.

After the initial icebreaker, give the panel a brief synopsis of your case. Like anyone else, jurors are susceptible to confirmation bias, meaning that they will make up their minds about the case very early on, and then assign more weight to the evidence that confirms their beliefs. So while they are still impressionable, you should take the opportunity to put a positive spin on your case. Here, you're setting the stage for the case you will put on later. But don't oversell it. If you hide all of the bad facts, for example, your opponent will undoubtedly highlight them and attack your credibility. One of the best lessons I've learned about credibility came from my pre-law-school days. As in law, one of the first rules of journalism is that if you report a story, you must fairly and accurately portray both sides. It's unfair to build up one side's story and make only positive claims if there is another side of the story or negative factors involved. Choose your statements carefully. Of course, you don't want to present the entire case for the opposing side. But avoid any statement or description that could be interpreted as overly partisan. Instead, focus on your two or three best facts and your two or three best responses to the other side. I work really hard at this stage to drop the adjectives and adverbs and describe my best facts as simply as possible, relying mainly on the subject and the verb.

Initially, the panel is going to be timid. So one way to get them to open up is by starting with simple yes-or-no questions that everyone will be able to answer. For example, ask if anybody knows any of the players involved. This includes you, your client, your opposing counsel, her client, or the judge. If your opponent has already done this, the venire should already be somewhat more talkative. But if you get the feeling that they're not, ask whether any of the venire members has been to a courthouse before. Almost all of them will have been, and it can segue into questions about their experiences, which in turn will tell you how trusting they are of the legal system. Always remember that you can ask the group a yes-or-no question, but questions to individuals should be open-ended.

Whenever you ask a question of the entire panel, ask it in a way that encourages a response. For example, start each general question with an engaging opening phrase, such as "How many of us feel . . . ?" or "How many agree that . . . ?" Also, raise your own hand and smile when you ask each question. This gesture invites people to raise their own hand and eases the tension associated with having the lone raised hand in a room full of strangers.

To save time, consider asking questions that will elicit the fewest raised hands. For every general question, you want to note the responses for the record. But if thirty people raise their hands and six don't, you're going to waste a lot of time making note of this. So ask the question in the negative. For example, consider the statement "Everyone deserves justice." Since you can expect that almost everyone will raise their hands if you ask if they agree with the statement, then the proper question would be "Who here *doesn't* think that everyone deserves justice?" If you think that a certain point of view is going to be so unpopular that certain panelists will not admit to it out of embarrassment, you can preface the question with a disclaimer. For example, you could start with, "Now there are a lot of people who believe . . ." or "Not everyone thinks that . . ." Potential jurors will be more likely to admit to a controversial belief if you acknowledge openly that they are not alone in believing it.

You should also break up your questions into groups. One way to introduce a new group of questions is to start with venire members whom you have identified as leaders or those who are unsympathetic. As discussed later in this chapter, you can ascertain which panel members fit into these groups by looking at the juror questionnaires or juror cards, or from responses that they give to other questions either by you or your opponent. So rather than ask a general question of the whole panel, ask a specific person how he feels about a certain topic. For example, "Mr. Smith, how do you feel about personal injury lawyers?"

As you pose your questions, remember that one of your main goals is to set up adverse jurors for causal strikes. One way to do this is by introducing a group of questions in a way that supports an adverse position. For example, suppose your case involves an acupuncturist, and your job is going to be to discredit the practice. During voir dire, then, you will want to root out those people who believe that acupuncture is a legitimate medical practice. So give the panelist a choice between a benign option that is against you and an extreme position in your favor. For example, "Mrs. Johnson, let's discuss acupuncture for a moment. Some people believe that it's a great alternative to traditional medicine for pain relief. Others believe that it's a quack science that never works. Which of these statements best describes how you feel about it?" Here, the language of the first option seems more attractive. But once the panelist adopts it, you have some support for a causal strike. A word of caution— when formulating the question, use language that is strong enough that supports a causal strike, but not so strong that the panelist would feel uncomfortable adopting it.

After the panel member adopts the adverse position, bind her to it so that it will be nearly impossible for your opponent to rehabilitate her. Ask a series of follow-up questions that suggest unfavorable answers. But don't stray too far afield. If you push the unfavorable juror too far, she may recognize that her ultimate position is absurd, which may lead her to recant. Once the juror adopts an adverse position, thank her for her opinion and summarize it for the rest of the venire. If they were paying attention, the other panel members will realize that the position your target has taken is against you. They will expect you to downplay that position. Rather, thank her for her honest responses and explain to the venire that the jury system just wouldn't work without such candor.

Now that you have set your expectations about honesty, you can seek out others who agree with the adverse position. To do this, loop that question into another general question for the entire panel. For example, "How many of us agree with Mrs. Johnson that acupuncture is the best alternative to traditional pain relief?" Looping answers back into questions has two benefits. The obvious benefit is that it helps you identify who else holds a belief that is against your position. But it also helps you identify which panel members are followers—that is, which of them are more likely to agree with a position only after someone else has stated it. Again, remember to phrase your question in a way that doesn't force other adverse panelists to take an extreme position. The choice they make has to be between two seemingly reasonable options.

When using the looping technique, you may find that some panelists hold views that are even more extreme than your original target. When this happens, roll that response into your looping to create a greater feeling of safety for potential jurors to admit a view or opinion adverse to your case. I do this by repeating my question and including the name of the second juror. For example, "Who else agrees with Mrs. Johnson and Mr. Smith that acupuncture is the best medicine?" The more peers who hold that position, the easier it is for other prospective jurors to admit to a similar opinion. There are strength and safety in numbers. Take advantage of this to wring all the information that you can out of potential jurors. As your looping flushes out other jurors with similar, adverse views, lock them into the extreme position. This will make it easier to find even more panelists who agree with the extreme view. In most courts, you typically won't make a causal challenge at this point. But when your opportunity to challenge does roll around, jurors who are locked in will have very little chance to escape the challenge.

Next, expand the discussion to the view that supports your case. Ask whether anybody disagrees with the position you've just been discussing. This is your opportunity to find supporters among the panel. If any of the people you identified as leaders disagrees with the adverse position, give them the floor. Let them respond to the adverse group in their own words. Again, there are two benefits to doing this. First, you are educating the entire panel about important issues through a neutral and detached venire person. The other panelists will trust this person because he doesn't have a dog in the fight. Second, it will help you to distinguish between the leaders and followers. If you're stuck with a leader in the jury room, better that it be a leader who will advocate for you.

Always remember that this is an adversarial process. Opposing counsel will know just as well as you do which panelists are favorable to you and which are not. He will try to challenge your best advocates and diminish the grounds for your challenges. As discussed above, your best bet for having your challenges sustained is to lock a prospective juror into an adverse position. In the same vein, your best bet for defeating challenges to your supporters is to inoculate them. You can do this by asking leading questions that tend to show this juror's ability to be fair. For example, assume that a juror sympathizes with your case because he went to an acupuncturist who could not relieve his pain at all. Your inoculation question can be "Even though acupuncture didn't help you very much, can you still be fair to both sides?" and "Can you promise that you'll fairly judge the evidence and follow the court's instructions?" Some lawyers will tell you to look for demographic information about your jurors. They claim that factors such as race, ethnicity, religion, sex, and income level can help you determine which way a juror will lean. Although this is true to some extent, relying too heavily on these factors can prove disastrous. I never assess a potential juror by demographics alone. Rather, I put a potential juror's demographic information into context with other information to paint a broader picture about that juror. I've also found that bias questions rarely uncover jurors' secret or unconscious biases. After all, how many people will admit to strangers that they are prejudiced or biased and hold grudges from past experiences? Instead, I keep track of information that is most helpful in determining who will make the best jurors for my client. The list[3] below lays out what I'm looking for in voir dire. This list is by no means set in stone. It changes depending on the type of case, the side I'm on, the venue, and so on. It also has a dual role—it's not only a list of things to look for in voir dire, but also a set of guidelines for formulating questions. Finally, remember that this list isn't a list of positives. Different cases call for different types of jurors. For example, a juror with certain preconceptions is only good if those preconceptions favor you or your client. So this list is simply a list of things to watch for. Make value judgments about potential jurors that fit into these categories in the context of the overall case.

Voir Dire Checklist

> *Preconceptions.* Does this juror have similar experiences to those of either party in this case? Does he have any knowledge or expertise relevant to this case? Most of the questions in voir dire should be geared toward discovering a potential juror's preconceptions.

> *Math and science.* Does this juror comprehend math and can he follow my expert? You should never assume anything about a juror's math skills. If you need jurors who are good at math, look for accountants or engineers. Alternatively, you can simply ask in voir dire, using any of the techniques discussed in this chapter.

> *Leadership.* Leadership comes in many shapes and sizes. A juror who would be a follower in one case may be a leader in another. There are a few factors you can look for to determine whether a juror will be a leader or a follower.

  ○ *Relevant knowledge.* Jurors naturally trust anyone with some level of expertise in an area, even if that person is not otherwise a natural leader.

  ○ *Employment and experience.* Lawyers, paralegals, and law students will be looked to for leadership by the rest of the jury.

---

3. *Adapted from* Back to Basics: Nine Things to Look for in Voir Dire, AMERICAN SOCIETY OF TRIAL CONSULTANTS, http://jurylaw.typepad.com/deliberations/12007/09/back'-to-basics-.html (Sept. 4, 2007, 14:53 EST).

Other professions that require natural leadership ability include business managers and teachers. Ask questions to seek out leadership roles at work and in personal activities.

○ *Age, sex, social class, education, and personality.* In my experience, the best inferences that can be drawn about demographic information have to do with leadership ability. Middle-aged male business managers tend to lead (and sometimes even control) jury deliberations. On the other hand, young blue-collar women tend to be followers.

❯ *Affinity.* Will this juror be likable? Will she like those around her, including me, my client, the judge, opposing counsel, his client, the other jurors? Factors to consider:

○ Personal chemistry.

○ Similar "life story."

○ Behaviors. Does this juror "buy local"? Drive a gas guzzler? Own dogs? Vote? Personal habits and behaviors can tell you a lot about whether they will like or dislike your client. If your client is a multinational farming conglomerate, for example, it might help to know that a particular juror only buys local.

❯ *Sense of control.* Does this juror believe in personal responsibility or that much of what happens to a person is a product of outside forces? Important questions include those about:

○ *Prior complaints.* Look for involvement in prior lawsuits, employment complaints, Better Business Bureau complaints, and insurance claims. If the judge would let me ask about sending back food at restaurants, I would ask, because I'm looking for people who quickly and willingly express dissatisfaction with the performance of others. I make a different choice, whether I am a plaintiff or a defendant, but a predisposition toward dissatisfaction or complaints usually signals a plaintiff-oriented juror. Likewise, jurors who have been sued or have had complaints lodged against them tend to be pro-defendant.

○ *Explanation of prior failures.* If the juror has been fired or her business has failed, how did she cope? Was it her fault or was her boss vindictive? Did she move on or file a complaint? Handle these questions with care as they tend to make people feel uncomfortable or even offended. But these are issues that go to the core of a potential juror's plaintiff or defendant bias.

○ *Supervisory and decision-making roles at work.* Managerial jobs necessarily require a belief in personal responsibility and self-control. In addition, they are associated with more flexible work schedules, so supervisors tend to be more autonomous and assume the same of others.

○ *Entrepreneurship, business ownership, and "self-made" success.* People who own or operate businesses are generally leaders or respected members of the community and as a result will have more persuasive power in the jury room.

○ *Future plans and expectations.* Jurors who have an elaborate life plan tend to have a stronger sense of personal responsibility and self-control.

○ *Age.* Some demographers suggest that Generation X jurors (born between the mid-'60s and late '70s) tend to believe in personal responsibility, while younger Generation Y jurors (born between the early '80s and mid-'90s) tend to have a sense of entitlement, blaming outside forces for their own problems.

○ *Physical strength or frailty.* A physically vital person will likely have a stronger sense of self-control than someone who is physically weak. Note that certain ailments might serve as a basis for causal strikes. I've heard of several cases in which jurors slept during testimony because of conditions that were not discovered during voir dire.

❯ *Story vs. process orientation.* Is this juror more inclined to listen to the stories told at trial, or to the technical aspects of the case, such as how a certain valve works in a product liability case, or how what constitutes causation in a negligence case?

○ *Style of expression. Story jurors* respond to questions with a narrative—"I believe X because five years ago, Y happened to me." *Process jurors* usually speak in the abstract, and answer questions more directly—"I believe X because Y is unfair."

○ *Profession.* Certain professions require the ability to tell stories to get a point across. These include sales, marketing, teaching, and counseling. Other professions require the ability to describe a process. Accountants, engineers, and computer programmers fall in this category. Some professionals, including doctors and lawyers, may have the ability to do both. If I'm struggling to type a juror, I ask myself how I would feel about defending this individual in a deposition. If I sense that he would take instruction and answer questions narrowly, that suggests a process juror (and a keeper). On the other hand, if I think I would be exhausted and frustrated because my advice would be ignored and I would need to constantly remind him to talk less, this would indicate a story juror and perhaps a leader. I would lean toward striking that one.

> *Identification with status quo.* Does this juror feel like a part of society or an outcast? Does she feel as though she "belongs"?
>   ○ *Work experience.* A *system juror* is likely to have held down a job at a large corporation for a long time. An *estranged juror*, on the other hand, is likely unemployed or has moved from job to job.
>   ○ *Affiliation with institutions.* Does the juror belong to community groups, church organizations, the PTA?

To the greatest extent possible, the lawyer should attempt to influence the jury pool selection. For plaintiff's counsel, it may be possible to file a lawsuit in any of several districts within a state, each of which may draw a substantially different jury pool. For employer's counsel, there often is the opportunity to remove state court actions to federal court based on federal question or diversity jurisdiction. Federal district courts generally draw jurors from a much different pool than do state courts. Federal court juries are generally viewed as more favorable for the defense because the jury pool is culled from a larger area and includes more affluent and conservative venire members. State court is frequently perceived to be more advantageous for plaintiffs, probably because the jury pool is more localized and because an urban or inner city population is regarded as more likely to be generous with a company's money than are rural jurors. Additionally, state court juries are frequently composed of twelve people instead of the usual six in federal court. With more jurors on the panel, there seems to be a greater tendency to compromise on a verdict, which usually does not inure to the benefit of a company. It's important for the lawyer to consider this "forum" issue at the outset of the litigation.

It's just as critical to discover as much as possible about the particular court and judge's jury selection process. Find out from the judge's law clerk whether or not a jury questionnaire can or will be used and, if so, whether you will be allowed to provide questions. Prepare specific questions for the questionnaire that elicit the information needed to identify the "ideal" juror for your type of case. Appendix A contains two sample jury questionnaires—one from an employment case and another from a securities case. Verify with the court's clerk the exact number of jurors in civil cases in that court, as well as the permitted number of peremptory strikes. Surprises in this area must be avoided. As early as possible, obtain a copy of the venire from which the jury will be chosen. This list typically contains very helpful identification and demographic information on each juror: name, address, marital status, educational background, occupation, residency, and so on. With this information, together with that gleaned from the juror questionnaires, you should prepare a juror profile sheet that ranks jurors in order of raw demographic desirability. Having immediate access to this information through use of a laptop computer in court can prove invaluable. Once in court, the time between voir dire and jury selection is very short. Thus, whatever you can prepare in advance will be very helpful. In districts that provide only the limited information of juror names in advance of trial, it's important to devise a system to help capture critical information while the jurors are responding to voir dire. It's also important to have cocounsel or a skilled paralegal at the table to assist while lead counsel actively conducts the voir dire.

Most important, though, is the admonition for you to watch and listen. You will find clues about jurors' beliefs not just by *what* they say, but also by *how* they say it. Pay attention to changes in body language and voice inflection. Is any juror avoiding eye contact with you? When one juror speaks, are any of the others nodding? What does their posture tell about what they're thinking? Pick up on any visual or aural cues you can about their predispositions and get a gut feeling for them. Also, you can use advanced techniques such as mirroring to make a juror feel more comfortable about opening up. Mirroring involves imitating a person's posture, gestures, and speech to build a rapport with him. For example, if a juror has a soft, quiet voice, bring down your own volume when talking to that juror. If a juror smiles at you, smile back.

Also, keep the verdict you want in mind. Your ideal juror may differ depending on the type of trial you're going to face. A juror who may be perfect for a trial on the merits may prove inadequate for a sentencing trial. Likewise, someone who has relevant work experience may be ideal for determining liability, but may award you less damages than you seek. Some lawyers suggest identifying ideal jurors through focus groups and mock trials, but much of what you will learn using these techniques you probably already know through common sense.

Remember that the end game is your closing argument. With that in mind, you'll want to know exactly how a particular judge will proceed to select jurors, including the number of peremptory strikes and the specific method the judge will employ. Remember, also, that some jurors can be struck for cause. Therefore, if a juror appears to be improperly predisposed one way or the other, he is subject to be stricken for cause. Any discussion regarding the striking of a juror should be conducted outside the presence and hearing of the jury panel to avoid antagonizing the subject juror or other potential jurors. Prepare in advance a voir dire witness seating chart that can be quickly completed at counsel's table. Handwritten charts also may be helpful, but may waste valuable time.

Take advantage of every minute with your jury, even during voir dire, by reinforcing the themes of your case into your questions. As you ask your questions, remember to admit and explain any weaknesses in your case. Your jurors will get the sense that you are being honest with them, which will build your credibility and reduce the impact that these weaknesses would otherwise have if the jury were surprised with them at trial. Admitting weaknesses will also allow you to candidly assess which jurors feel strongly about them, and you can use this information as a basis for causal challenges.

As you go through voir dire, there are two personality traits that you have to be very careful of—reluctance and eagerness. Reluctant jurors are usually sheep, but for the wrong reasons. They will vote with the majority often for the sake of expedience. This is not always a bad thing, especially if the majority of the jurors is leaning in your favor. But remember that a reluctant juror generally is a poor juror. Eager jurors are much worse. They may have an agenda and will be good about hiding it if they know how the system works (that is, if they know they'll be challenged for expressing a biased view). Eager jurors are often unhappy about the justice system generally or a particular issue specifically. So you must identify these types of feelings at voir dire or risk an unhappy juror tainting your case.

I generally try to exclude leaders, because once you put a leader in the jury box, that leader might end up steering everyone against you. I view myself as the leader in the courtroom, so I try to pick jurors who will follow me. For similar reasons, I stay away from jurors who are particularly experienced in the issues at the heart of the lawsuit. For example, try to stay away from doctors in a medical malpractice case or construction workers in a case involving a construction site accident. Rather, you want jurors who are willing to learn about the issues and can pay attention throughout the trial.

As you are weeding out the unfavorable jurors, pay special attention to their sensibilities. If you offend a panelist in voir dire, and that person winds up serving on the jury, you will be fighting an uphill battle through trial trying to regain her confidence. So formulate your questions carefully, and never ask a question that you haven't vetted in advance. I once saw a lawyer question a prospective juror who admitted to watching a fair number of law-related television shows. The lawyer asked whether that person could separate fiction from reality in the courtroom. The potential juror was offended, making it very difficult for the lawyer ever to gain his trust again. It's pointless to try to change people or their attitudes. You'll never get a juror to come over to your way of thinking. Instead, the case must be positioned in a way that is congruent with the person's beliefs.

Conclude by asking the panel, generally, if there is any reason, already mentioned or not, why any member could not be a totally fair, impartial, and unprejudiced juror. This question sums up the whole purpose of a jury trial and the voir dire examination. If the judge allows it, you can also tell the jurors that if there are any particularly sensitive issues that you should know about, they can raise those issues with you, opposing counsel, and the judge in private.

Time-Saving Techniques

Below is a list of techniques that will help you save time in voir dire:

a. **Keep your introduction short.** Three minutes should be
    enough time to introduce yourself, your client, and the basic
    issues that you're going to discuss. Voir dire is the only opportu-
    nity you get to have a conversation with the jurors, so get them
    talking early.

b. **Give the jurors some ground rules at the beginning.** Let them know that the people up front will get most of the questions because they're most likely to be chosen.

c. **Learn basic information by using juror questionnaires or juror cards.** It's a waste of everyone's time to have each juror tell you basic information about themselves, such as where they live and whether they're married.

d. **Set a time line for your questions.** Know in advance how much time you have and divide the total time by the number of issues you need to discuss. The result is the average amount of time each issue should take, but you can adjust the time for each issue based on its importance.

e. **Control talkative jurors.** As a part of your introduction, let the jurors know that you have to give everyone an opportunity to respond. This way, a potential juror will be less offended when you have to cut his time short. If you have to do this, be polite—thank him for his contribution, but let him know that you noticed other people raise their hands in response to a question and you want to hear from them as well.

f. **Limit the number of questions you ask of each juror.** Don't focus your attention only on those jurors you think you will strike. If everyone raises their hands on a particular issue, you may not have time to hear from all of them on that issue. But make sure you go back to those people next time they raise their hands. You don't want any of the venire to feel as though their contribution is not important.

g. **Pose questions in the alternative.** As discussed above, this will help you root out adverse jurors. But it can also help you save time by framing the issue for the entire panel.

At the end of voir dire, make sure that you have the opportunity to absorb all of the information that you have gathered before making your ultimate selections. If necessary, ask the judge for a few moments to review your notes on the jurors before the actual selection process begins. Any amount of time the court permits can be put to effective use, particularly if your notes are organized. Remember that your primary goal in jury selection is to deselect, through the use of peremptory strikes (or for-cause dismissal), those jurors who you believe will be most likely to hurt your case. Jurors are human beings who bring to court all of their predispositions based on their experiences, their exposures, and their religious, political, economic, and philosophical beliefs. Specifically, the types of jobs jurors hold, their educational backgrounds, and their similarities or empathy with a party in the case or a party's counsel are powerful factors that may result in partiality. These are all important in deciding whom to strike. The lawyer should visualize prior to trial what the characteristics are of the jurors she does not want, and then utilize peremptory strikes accordingly.

2. Challenging Jurors for Cause

Every jurisdiction has special rituals or "magic words" that must be used to perfect a challenge for cause, but over the years, I've developed the following list to help me nail down a for-cause challenge:

> Step 1: If a juror states a strong opinion that gives rise to a challenge for cause, start by repeating the juror's answer: "Let me make sure I understand what you are saying . . ."

> Step 2: Next, probe the reason for his opinion. Ask him why he feels this way. But bear in mind that this, and only this, is the appropriate time to ask open-ended questions in a challenge for cause.

> Step 3: As you conduct your challenge for cause, after the one "why" question, always ask closed-ended questions. Never ask a direct question about a juror's bias. Rather, soften the blow with wishy-washy language. Notice how the italicized part of each question below softens the impact of the question:[4]

 ○ You would agree with me that you feel pretty strongly about this issue?

 ○ *Would it be fair to say that* you've felt this way for a long time?

> You can also analogize the case to a competition and ask if the other side would have a bit of an advantage:

 ○ Given what you said before, would the defendant *start with a bit of an edge?*

 ○ Would the plaintiff have *a little steeper hill to climb* to prove its case?

---

4. Example questions *adapted from* TRIAL BEHAVIOR CONSULTING, THEME DEVELOPMENT AND JURY SELECTION IN PRODUCT LIABILITY LITIGATION (Feb. 2000), http://trialbehavior.com/articles/Theme Development and Jury Selection in Product Liability Litigation.htm.

○ Would the defendant be *starting a little bit behind* the plaintiff?

○ *If this trial were a race,* would we be starting one step behind?

❯ Step 4: After the juror has admitted to some level of bias, you then have to raise (and solidify against rehabilitation) the level of commitment. Ask questions such as:

○ So, even if the evidence calls for it, you feel that you probably could not vote in favor of . . . ?

○ So, even if the Court instructed you as to the law on this issue, you believe you would be unable to vote in favor of . . . ?

○ I don't like oysters. When I was young my mother told me I would like them, but I didn't. Today, no matter how many experts tell me oysters taste good—and even if a nutritionist told me oysters are great to build strong bones and healthy teeth—I still don't and won't like oysters. That is what we mean by a bias or prejudice being a strong opinion that is not likely to change. So, would it be fair to say that on the issue of [. . .], you would start the trial with a prejudgment or strong opinion that lawyers refer to as a bias or prejudice? Would you agree that this prejudgment or bias is so much a part of you that it would prevent you from giving a fair judgment on our side of the case?

○ Do you feel that in this case, with your strong feelings on the issue of [. . .], you would not be an impartial and fair judge of some parts of this case?

○ So, would it be fair to say that no matter whether it was me or the judge or someone else who asked you to leave that opinion aside, you feel so strongly about this, you would not be able to set your opinion aside on this issue?

In closing, there is no single formula for you to follow. You must consider how each of the factors outlined in this chapter plays into your case. People are complicated; they come from a variety of backgrounds and their beliefs often clash with the beliefs of those around them. And there's no magic spell you can cast that will make them agree with you. Rather, the techniques in this chapter will help you select those jurors who will agree with you, deselect those who won't, and maintain your credibility throughout the process. Once you've selected and sworn your jury, you are ready to move on to the main focus of this book—presenting your case to the "modern juror."

CHAPTER 3

The Science of the Brain as It Relates to Trial Presentations

> "Memory is a net; full of fish when taken from the brook, but a dozen miles of water have run through it without sticking."
>
> —*Oliver Wendell Holmes*

The power of a trial presentation resides in the lawyer's ability to tell an interesting, persuasive, and credible story. Jurors become bored and lose interest in a trial because the lawyers overwhelm them with more information than the human mind can handle. In the storm of evidence that a trial can become, story lines become lost, and the path is lost. Jurors unable or unwilling to muddle through will shut down. If the juror can't easily comprehend and retain the information, she'll ignore it and replace it with something she understands, connects to, and remembers, and it may be something you'll wish she had never heard.

An effective lawyer tells a story in simple terms that a juror can understand: one that captures a juror's attention and completes the second phase of winning over the jury—an emotional connection. Once that connection with your client and your story is made, the jurors will work harder to follow your evidence and learn how to use it to render a verdict in your client's favor.

A common issue is that typical trial lawyers offer thousands of words, hundreds of documents, and tangled diagrams and charts, causing the brain to switch off. Have you ever used a demonstrative chart that looks like this?

Shareholder Derivative Process

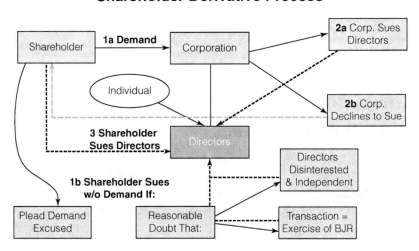

If so, I can almost guarantee that your jurors are suffering from a reaction I call "Juror Overload." The jury has been hit with far too much new data for their brains to process. They become so confused and overwhelmed that their overloaded information receptors literally shut down and shut off the flow of incoming information. It is no different than locking up your computer trying to process too much data at once. And just as you lost that document you were working on when your computer locked up, you will lose any goodwill or emotional connection you were building.

I promise you that when the jurors' minds reboot, they don't jump back into your trial presentation and fight to catch up. Instead, their minds drift to the problems and puzzles that occupy their own lives: "Is it time to get an oil change?" Or, "I wonder what's for dinner tonight?" Juror Overload causes your evidence and arguments to fall on deaf ears. When that happens, your entire reason for being there is gone. Bad trial presentations confuse the jury, lose their attention, and persuade no one.

The price of Juror Overload is ineffective communication. Juror Overload is toxic to you, your client, and ultimately your case. If the jury doesn't understand your opening or is bored by your closing, you've lost precious persuasion time. Forever.

Juror Overload is supported by research that encourages us to modernize our presentations and align our techniques to the way people learn.

In Chapter 1, you learned that in today's fast-paced world, it's vital that you design your courtroom presentations to be compatible with how people learn and manage attention. Scientists learn more every day about how the mind works. In his book *Multimedia Learning*,[1] Richard Mayer of the University of California–Santa Barbara offers an overview of human cognitive processing.

Since the 1990s, Mayer has conducted research studies on multimedia learning that studied combining words and pictures to achieve optimal understanding and retention. The studies have resulted in clear recommendations for multimedia design principles. This research can be applied in the courtroom. It teaches us how to communicate most effectively based on the way the human mind works.

Human beings possess a visual processing system and verbal information processing system.[2] The visual system processes information presented to the eyes (such as images, movies, and text). The verbal system processes information presented to the ears (such as words or nonverbal sounds). But, there are limits on our ability to process information. As a result, we must pick and choose which processing system—visual or verbal—to use. In short, the mind can only receive on one frequency at a time. However, both frequencies are essential in building a more complete understanding of any given topic.

This is research that has been echoed throughout the scientific community. In volume 12 of *The Handbook of Psychology*,[3] Irving Weiner cites a study Mayer conducted in 2001. After learning how a scientific system worked (such as the brakes on a car), students were tested for understanding. Students who both listened to a lesson and saw visual aids retained more information than those who only listened. This is called the "multimedia effect." It's engaging both the left and right sides of the brain.

Have you ever had a profound idea in the middle of the night or while in the shower or at the beach? When you're relaxed and not focused on a task, your left brain shuts down and your right brain takes over, allowing creativity and ideas to come to you. When you look at

1. Richard E. Mayer, Multimedia Learning (2001).
2. Richard E. Mayer and Roxana Moreno. A Cognitive Theory of Multimedia Learning: Implications for Design Principles.
3. 12 Irving B. Weiner, The Handbook of Psychology (2003).

a piece of abstract art, you're using your right brain and looking at the colors and lines of the art, but when you critique a piece of art, your left brain kicks in and you look for flaws or specific techniques. When you learn to use both sides of your brain equally—admiring the colors and creativity while identifying techniques—it brings the art to life and you can visualize it with your eyes closed. This is the mental process you want to tap in your jurors. You want them to be able to understand your case by appreciating and remembering the relationship between abstract arguments and the specific factual details. As a trial lawyer, you must be mindful of this and create a trial presentation that presents complementary material in both words and pictures. The visuals you present must complement what you're saying, so that they support your words rather than compete with them for the jury's attention.

Abraham Lincoln wasn't being complimentary when he said of Maclean, "He can compress the most words into the smallest idea of any man I know."[4] Your jury should not have to search through a visual or factual haystack to find the needle that you're talking about. People have a limited capacity to process and retain information. Simply put, we can only hold so much in our minds before we reach our limit. You've no doubt had the experience of overloading your computer by trying to download a large file. The computer slows down. Impatient, you try to switch to another program while the download progresses, but the computer won't respond to your mouse. The windows all sort of freeze, and you can't accomplish anything. A similar sequence happens when we ask too much of the human brain. If we're asked to take in more complex information than our brains can handle, we often give up trying.

Regardless of whether the input is visual or verbal, our mind can only process so much information. If you present images quickly or jumbled, the mind cannot keep up. Therefore, images must be organized in a way that will support, reinforce or summarize the spoken information. Don't use a PowerPoint slide if all you are going to do is quote the slide verbatim. When a narration is presented, the listener can only hold a few words in working memory at any one time. "A jury," as Vincent Bugliosi once said, "remembers the tune but not the words."[5] In the courtroom, the trial lawyer must always keep in mind the limited capacity of the brain to pro-

---

4. The Quotations Page, http://www.quotationspage.com/quote/1354.html.
5. Vincent Bugliosi is an attorney and author best known for prosecuting Charles Manson and other defendants accused of the Tate-LaBianca murders. His most recent books are *Reclaiming History: The Assassination of John F. Kennedy* (2007), and *The Prosecution of George W. Bush for Murder* (2008).

cess new information and must minimize the chances of overloading the cognitive system. The Rule of Three states that juries can only hold three major groups of information in their heads at a time. This information is then processed through three steps: (1) receive the material presented; (2) organize the material; and (3) integrate the material with prior experiences and knowledge. Jurors are programmed to process and make sense of the information they are presented. As trial lawyers we cannot change this. Instead, we adapt our presentations by selecting, organizing and integrating our evidence to make it easy for the jurors to process. The best trial lawyers help jurors filter, organize, and manage evidence and arguments so as to reach the conclusion most favorable to their clients.

Through the lens of *The Attention Economy*,[6] we can refine how we frame the challenge that faces trial lawyers today: How do we change our communication styles and techniques to compete for jurors' attention? We can learn new techniques from experts in education, marketing, and broadcast news.

One logical place to look for answers is in the classroom and the common-sense teaching techniques used by educators who deal with children who have difficulty focusing their attention. My mother is a first-grade teacher and reading therapist with 30 years of experience working with children with attention-deficit challenges. She tells me that most children with ADD are quite intelligent (as are our jurors). The problem is that the child is literally so distracted by all the other issues shooting through his mind that the message never reaches that intelligent child. ADD does not impair a student's ability to pay attention. Instead, it affects the ability to control *where* one is paying attention.

I spent a lot of time listening to and learning from my mother about the techniques that good teachers employ to combat ADD symptoms and focus distractible children. I'm grossly oversimplifying the great work my mother does with these children, but it essentially boils down to making learning concise, interactive, and fun. Trial lawyers should take a page out of the ADD teacher's lesson plans and apply these same ideas to focus distractible jurors.

Let me be clear. The point is not for attorneys to understand the clinical ins and outs of attention disorders. Whether a juror really has ADD is irrelevant. The idea is that in today's fast-paced, sound-bite,

6. THOMAS H. DAVENPORT & JOHN C. BECK, THE ATTENTION ECONOMY: UNDERSTANDING THE NEW CURRENCY OF BUSINESS (2001).

30-second grab-and-go world, we're all distracted by the vast amounts of information we receive and decisions we face each day. We've all become accustomed to receiving information quickly and moving on. Let's face it, communications media outside the courtroom have adapted, but the flow of information inside the courtroom remains overwhelming and inaccessible. Jurors become easily bored, confused, and frustrated.

It seems that marketing companies and media are taking their cue from teachers. The marketing focus is on obtaining and maintaining attention. Marketing executives teach us that a message has to be "sticky" to achieve the sale—or in our case, the decision in our client's favor. In *The Tipping Point*[7] by Malcolm Gladwell, he explains the concept of a sticky message with examples from Sesame Street and Blues Clues. According to Gladwell, Sesame Street became sticky despite the fact that it was an educational program because of the addition of Big Bird, who communicated and interacted with live actors. Blues Clues used a simple concept of the main character speaking to the camera and then pausing after each question. A simple pause captures the audience's attention as if he's speaking directly to them. Gladwell points out that stickiness isn't based on the volume of our voices or the emphasis we put on certain words. It can be something as simple as a giant, yellow, talking bird or a pause, something unexpected that can "tip the point" in your favor.

Another lesson from marketers is in the choice of words we use to present our cases. Think of the commercials that simply state "Got milk?" or "Where's the beef?" These short phrases are simple, catchy, and memorable.

When preparing for a case, create key phrases or "case slogans" that will be memorable and capture a jury's attention such as "trusted to his care, custody, and control" when presenting a case on child endangerment or neglect. In a recent trademark case I tried, the defendant testified that the numerous similarities between their website and the plaintiff's product presentation were "coincidence." My case slogan in that trial quickly became "Coincidence. Really?" My point was twofold: there were too many similarities to be a coincidence, and the defendant was lying. It will take a generation to forget the late Johnnie Cochran's O.J. exonerating phrase, "If it doesn't fit, you must acquit."

---

7. MALCOLM GLADWELL, THE TIPPING POINT: HOW LITTLE THINGS CAN MAKE A BIG DIFFERENCE (2000).

Also, opening with a question engages the jury and gives them a sense of connection with your case. Following are a few examples of question openers:

> ❯ When was the last time you . . .
> ❯ Did you know that . . .
> ❯ Do you ever ask yourself . . .
> ❯ How many times have you said to yourself . . .
> ❯ Are you tired of hearing stories about . . .
> ❯ Who can put a price on . . .

In short, make your presentation sticky, memorable, and personal to engage the jury whenever possible. Once you capture their attention, keep it by reminding the jury from time to time about what woke them up. However, use your judgment, because you can overuse a slogan. No matter how catchy it is, overuse can cause your jurors to tune out or become annoyed. As with everything, balance is key.

If you take into account how our mental processes operate, you can help your jury easily understand and retain material. Conversely, if you ignore key facts about your jury's mental processes and capacity limitations, you'll quickly overwhelm or confuse them. You must design your trial presentation so that the facts of your case are understood and remembered by the jury. The tangle of evidence presented at trial (documents, testimony, demonstratives, and arguments) can quickly overload jurors' cognitive systems if you're not careful. You must help the jury to select, organize, and integrate the information you present. You can accomplish this by designing a trial presentation that incorporates both visual and verbal forms of information. To make your key points even more memorable, present them one at a time. An example of this concept is illustrated in the media.

How often do you watch your local news? Daily? Weekly? More than once a day? Have you ever noticed that with both the local and national news channels, news repeats, unless breaking news interrupts the loop? Have you ever wondered how producers can get through an entire world's worth of news in 30 minutes and not change up the next segment but loop the news from the earlier segment? Producers must look at all the news of the day from every corner of the world and then decide which pieces are most relevant to their audience. Trial lawyers need to do the same thing—cull through all the facts of the trial and pinpoint those facts that are most relevant to the jury's decision in favor of your client, and focus on those facts so that the jurors don't become confused or overwhelmed with unnecessary information. In Chapter 4, we'll take a closer look at the Seven Principles of effective jury communication.

CHAPTER 4

A Closer Look at the Seven Principles

> "Principles have no real force except
> when one is well-fed."
>
> —*Mark Twain*

In Chapter 1, I introduced the seven principles for communicating effectively with the jury. In this chapter we'll look at each in more depth, and then in Chapters 5 through 14 we'll explore some very practical, step-by-step actions you can take at each phase of trial.

Remember, communication is a participatory activity. It's not enough for you to present information. The information must be received and processed, and that will happen only if you get and keep the jury's attention. Using the seven principles to design a clear and compelling trial presentation, you'll connect with your jury, hold their attention, and promote their understanding and memory of the facts of your case.

Each of the seven principles draws on scientifically proven facts about our mental processes. The principles apply at every level of scale, from the presentation as a whole all the way down to individual illustrations of a single slide and the design of text.

1. The Personal Credibility Principle: *Demonstrate competence, accuracy, leadership, and efficiency to gain credibility.*

Every time you move, speak, or breathe before a jury, your credibility is at stake. Yes, I mean every time you do anything before a jury. Jurors flyspeck your every move for clues to your competence and trustworthiness. If you appear lost and confused, you'll lose their trust. If your opponent is better able to move exhibits into evidence efficiently, the situation is even worse for you and your client. On the other hand, if you move through the evidence efficiently with confidence and demonstrate a mastery of the facts, the jury will surrender their attention to you because you're a leader in the courtroom.

Because the jury is watching, you must, in every action, send the implicit message that you are confident and that you have something accurate and material to say and will say it as efficiently as possible. Never waste the jury's valuable time with the inconsequential. I can't tell you how many times I've interviewed jurors after a trial and heard one of the following:

> "The other lawyer kept making the same points over and over."
> "The trial should have been three days shorter."

Remember, jurors are people too. They have lives, wives, husbands, kids, and jobs to which they must return. Don't insult or antagonize them. By wasting their time, you also destroy your own credibility. In Chapter 5, we'll examine techniques to increase your credibility with your jury.

2. The Road Map Principle: *People learn better when the material is presented with clear outlines and headings.*

Preview case themes and ideas so jurors will know what they're looking for. Structure and core themes help jurors decide in your favor because you're teaching them what's important in the case. Consider this opening statement from a recent contract dispute trial:

> This case will require you to decide whether an oral contract existed between the plaintiff, Mr. Alexander, and the defendant, Mr. Dalton. During the course of this trial, I will prove three facts that demonstrate that the parties entered into an oral partnership to develop a low-income residential housing project called "Casas del Sol": First, I will prove Mr. Dalton has a history of oral agreements and business deals; second, I will prove Mr. Alexander and Mr. Dalton acted like partners in operating Casas del Sol; and third, I will prove Mr. Dalton and Mr. Alexander have a history of business dealings based on an oral agreement and trust.

Before the jury is assaulted with 15 witnesses they've never met, the numerous moving parts in a real estate development, the complications of the statute of frauds, as well as any diversionary tactics employed by the defense, you must orient them in time and space and tell them explicitly what's really important in the case and how you plan to organize the information for them. Establish a routine and give oral signposts to explain what you're doing and how you intend to proceed. After having a new witness introduce himself to the jury, I will follow up with a broad question such as "Mr. Smith, can you tell the jury what your relationship is to this case?" Answer: "I am a personal friend of Plaintiff and heard Defendant promise one-half of the profits in the Casas del Sol development to Plaintiff."

From the start, the jurors know this witness's relationship to the parties and the general subject matter of his testimony. If a witness takes the stand and gets asked the normal questions about where he grew up, if he is married, and his level of education, the jury has no idea whether you are qualifying this witness as an expert or establishing his credentials as a reliable family man. The more comfortable the jurors are with their surroundings and where you're heading, the more they can focus on and listen to your message. We have all had the experience of stumbling to the bathroom in the dark or trying to find the light switch in dark unfamiliar hotel room. Is it fun? Is it a good learning environment? No. So, turn the lights on and give your jury clear guidance in the form of transition sentences and signposts. These techniques will help you set juror expectations and manage juror focus. In Chapter 8, we'll look at techniques you can use to help jurors filter information and combine the techniques with case themes at all the different phases of a trial.

3. The Chunking Principle: *People learn better when information is presented in bite-sized chunks.*

Grouping information to make it more easily understood is known as "chunking". When it comes to your message at trial, the salesman's rule of K.I.S.S. should apply: Keep It Short and Simple. When a message becomes too complicated, jurors won't simply try harder to understand. Instead, Juror Overload will rear its dazed and confused head. Their minds will block you out. Even worse, they'll blame you, the supposed professional advocate, for not being smart enough or good enough to clearly communicate your message.

In those situations, you lose jurors' attention and create an even greater challenge for yourself later. Do you think a juror will be eager to tune back in the next time you stand to speak? Not likely. You've failed to prove yourself a worthy leader in the courtroom. In Chapter 9, we'll draw on the "chunking" principle first introduced in 1956 by Harvard psychologist George A. Miller to learn how to break your evidence into manageable and memorable chunks.

4. The Multimedia Principle: *People learn better from words and pictures than from words alone.*

Science supports the commonsense conclusion that multimedia evidence makes a presentation more memorable. McGraw-Hill published the Weiss-McGrath Report in 1992, which compared retention of information presented orally, visually, and both orally and visually. The study is of particular use to trial lawyers because it tested memory after 72 hours, which is about the length of a short trial. The study revealed that participants who were presented information orally only retained about 10% of the information, while the participants who only received information visually doubled the retention rate to 20%. However, the most dramatic results were seen in the participants who received the information both orally and visually. Those participants retained an eye-popping 65% of the information they were presented.

The study reinforces the idea that individuals presented with both visual and oral information understand it better and retain it longer. Plus, the communication and interaction with the jury becomes more interesting and engaging with a demonstration or a chart. Seeing is believing, and it is far better for a juror to see something with his own eyes than simply rely on something the lawyer or a witness says is true.

By the way, does the following chart help crystallize my point?

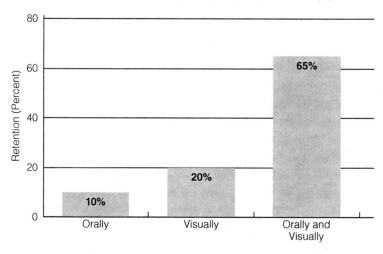

In a recent study, students were asked to walk down a hall and take a test, but not before they were shown words such as age, wrinkle, slow down, and gray. These words reportedly sank into the unconscious minds of the students as they walked slowly down the hallway. Another group of students was tested with words like quick, fast, youthful, and dynamic. As you may have already guessed, students rushed down the hallway. A final group was tested with words such as hurry up, impatient, and impulsive. Researchers were not surprised to witness students exhibiting rude, less courteous behaviors. The unconscious mind is a powerful tool and through the proper use of multimedia exhibits, it can give you the upper hand.

In Chapter 10, we'll look at how to enhance the persuasiveness of your openings, closings, and examinations through the use of multimedia presentations.

5. The "Less Is More" Principle: *People learn better when extraneous material is excluded.*

Communication is most effective when neither too much nor too little information is presented. In all my years of practice, I have never once heard a juror complain that a trial was too short. I would be willing to bet a lot of money that my experiences are not unique and no juror has ever wished for "just one more witness," much less another day of testimony.

Accordingly, the "less is more" principle has two main aspects. First, the trial presentation must be built from the outset around the desired verdict. Every aspect of the presentation should be relevant to what you want your jury to know and conclude when they walk into the jury room to deliberate.

Second, the jury should be told only what they must know to reach your verdict: telling them too little will leave them puzzled, and telling them too much will leave them overwhelmed, disoriented, and irritated (and ultimately bored because they'll stop trying to track what you're saying). Telling jurors irrelevant facts is like explaining how to build a clock after someone asks you for the time.

Allow me to share a demonstrative story. Two men set out in a boat to go fishing one morning. The fog rolled in and the men lost sight of the shoreline. When the fog receded, the two men saw an unfamiliar coastline, but came across a fisherman. One of the men in the boat yelled to the fisherman on the shore, "Where are we?" The man on the shore yelled back, "You are in a boat." The man in the boat turned to his companion and said, "That guy on the shore is a lawyer." His companion asked, "How do you know that?" He replied, "The information he gave us is totally accurate, but totally useless."

Eliminating the extraneous starts with the small stuff. For example, keep your trial table neat, uncluttered, and free from distraction. I've seen jurors spend entire examinations on the edge of their seats watching to see if opposing counsel would knock over his Diet Coke as he swung his arms recklessly to emphasize points. The jury never even heard his words because they were so distracted by the soda sideshow.

Eliminating the extraneous includes the big ideas as well. Use the Rule of Three and limit yourself to three big themes that are clear, simple, and uncluttered. (After all, the Rule of Three teaches that jurors can only hold three ideas in their mind at one time.) Chapter 11 will focus on techniques to keep your message crisp and clean.

6. The Stickiness Principle: *Make your themes and ideas "sticky."*

In their book *Made to Stick: Why Some Ideas Survive and Others Die*,[1] Dan and Chip Heath describe the qualities that make certain ideas stick in people's minds. Their book continues the idea of "stickiness" popularized by Malcolm Gladwell in *The Tipping Point*.[2] As discussed earlier, an idea can be simple and still be unexpected. If our themes, arguments, and evidence create a lasting impression, they'll change jurors' opinions and behavior. Use multisensory techniques to bring your ideas and themes to life, and they will *stick* with the audience long after you sit down. Visual aids work, so use them. It's vital to connect the dots because people absorb only what they understand.

The multisensory concept involves incorporating as many senses as possible into a presentation. These senses include sight, smell, taste, touch, and sound.

---

1. Dan Heath & Chip Heath, Made to Stick: Why Some Ideas Survive and Others Die (2d ed. 2008).
2. Malcolm Gladwell, The Tipping Point: How Little Things Can Make a Big Difference (2000).

With dyslexic students, teachers use materials that can be manually manipulated to implant into the child's memory the process of shaping a letter. Easily molded objects such as pudding or sand are placed in a box or a bowl and the child is instructed to draw the letter in the sand while naming it and verbalizing it. This process of learning integrates three of the child's senses: sound, sight, and touch. Teachers have found that the more senses they can activate in the learning process, the better the child is able to understand and remember the lesson.

During trial presentation, a creative attorney can use multisensory evidence to his or her advantage. For example, if your case involves pollution, a sample of polluted, putrid-smelling, off-color water would be memorable to the jury. In the movie *Erin Brockovich*, which was based on a true case of pollution in California in which millions were given in a settlement after residents of a town grew sick or died after being exposed to polluted water, Ms. Brockovich made her point by bluffing that the water had been imported from the affected town's water supply.

If your case involves mental anguish, let the jury hear the anguish. (I don't know if this is legal, just throwing out ideas.) When delivering bad news to your client, record his or her initial reaction to the news and play it back for the jury. Often, by the time a case goes to trial, the original anguish and pain are gone from your client and the actions won't be as raw and real as when they were fresh. Any time you can incorporate the sounds of real emotions, you'll have a better chance of grabbing your jury's attention. Chapter 12 will go further in depth on ways that you can use emotions, stories, and other techniques to make your points memorable in court.

7. The Jolt Principle: *Periodically jolt your jury so they do not bolt.*

It's difficult to sustain high levels of interest in any topic for an extended period of time. (I'm pleased and impressed that you've read this far through the book.) We all need to take a short break to relax and refocus our thoughts. Most successful TV shows are designed with this in mind and contain carefully planned peaks and valleys along with rich textures of emotion and excitement that highlight what audiences are to remember and lowlight what it's okay to forget. The peak of each mountain indicates a moment of emphasis, a moment of dramatic tension. The polar opposite of this tension is the valley, a moment of relaxation. Without these peaks and valleys, a TV show will feel monotonous and uncompelling, even if every moment is supposed to be exciting. So plan your trial with periodic jolts to reignite the jury's interest.

As trial lawyers, we're taught on day one of our Trial Advocacy class the concepts of primacy and recency. Juror attention is highest when you make your first and last points. In the beginning, the jury listens in order to answer the question: Why are we here? In the end, the jurors perk up again and listen to hear you summarize the main points they missed because they drifted off in the middle. The drifting-off-in-the-middle phenomenon is so common that most lawyers take it for granted, gathering their best points at the beginning and the end. It's as if we stuff our jury into a bottle, toss them out to sea, and then wait for the tide to bring them back for our summation. But why do that to them? Look at it this way: The jury's there and you're there. It's foolish to waste a single minute of the time you have with them. To keep your jury from drifting off in the middle, you need to jolt them from time to time. This means doing or saying something that significantly changes the pace of your presentation or examination. It could be:

> Projecting an important exhibit through trial presentation software
> Moving from the podium to a flip chart
> Giving a verbal signpost that you're changing subjects
> Using a picture or graph
> Asking the witness a question that seeks an explanation of a major factual dispute

Jolting requires only that you do something different in the midst of your presentation or examination. In Chapter 13, we'll explore "jolting" and the science behind it in more detail and provide some real-world examples of how to jolt in both your arguments and examinations.

As Ralph Waldo Emerson stated, "All great speakers were bad speakers at first." There are some who believe that outstanding trial lawyers are born talented and that all the training in the world couldn't equal that innate ability. I disagree. A transcript of Martin Luther King Jr.'s grades from Crozier Theological Seminary shows he received his lowest grade in public speaking, a C. As you know, he went on to become one of the greatest public speakers of his time.[3]

Like great speakers, great trial lawyers aren't born. They're built through hard work, study, and practice. In the book *Talent Is Overrated*,[4] Geoff Colvin says that the primary difference between the "good" and the "great" is practice and persistence.

But, frankly, it doesn't matter whether you achieve greatness, as long as you continue to improve throughout your career. Without question, we can all become better trial lawyers than we are today. I'm not finished evolving, and my guess is that if you're reading this book, you aren't either. The things I've learned, I've learned the hard way. As my dad says, "Experience is a tough teacher: it gives the exam first and the lesson later." By making a lot of mistakes and spending quite a few years getting my nose bloodied in courts across Texas, I've improved as a trial lawyer and discovered there are real, tangible techniques that have made me better at it. I share them with you because I truly believe these techniques form the foundation of a better way to try a case and reach juries with your client's story. As I tell my trial advocacy students at the start of each semester, my goal is to help you become a better trial lawyer. And that is the sole focus of this book.

---

3. Charles V. Willie, Richard J. Riddick & Ronald Brown, The Black College Mystic 108 (2006).
4. Geoff Colvin, Talent Is Overrated: What Separates World-Class Performers from Everybody Else (2008).

CHAPTER 5

The Personal Credibility Principle: Demonstrate Competence, Integrity, and Efficiency to Gain Credibility

> "Credibility is like virginity. Once you lose it,
> you can never get it back."
>
> —*Unknown*

As discussed in Chapter 2, your ability to convince the jury that you are credible can determine the outcome of your case. If they perceive you as trustworthy and your opponent as less so, then he will be fighting an uphill battle throughout the trial, even if the legal burden rests with you. And if they trust you, then by extension they trust your client.

Credibility is by far the most important principle in this book because it is the foundation of our trade. If you don't have it, your chances of winning over a jury are slim to none. So let's begin.

1. The Credibility Gap

Throughout trial, the jurors will weigh the difference between what they hear from you and what they perceive to be the truth. This is the credibility gap. Your goal in trial should be to close the gap by the time you close the case. That is, when you get up to deliver your closing argument, the jury should already perceive you as the most credible person in the room. It's important to establish credibility *before* closing, because that last phase of trial is where credibility becomes the most powerful tool you have. If the jury finds you credible, then even your weakest arguments will pass muster.

In this section, I will discuss the credibility gap and how it relates to the trial. But as an initial matter, notice that the credibility gap is not the difference between what you *say* and what the truth *is*. Rather it's the difference between what the jurors *hear* and what they *perceive* to be the truth. This distinction is vastly important.

To understand why, consider the motion in limine. By waiting until the middle of trial to raise an evidentiary objection, you're putting yourself in a lose-lose situation. On the one hand, you're risking a spot decision by the judge, who may overrule your objection and let the evidence in. But even if you prevail on the objection, your credibility will nevertheless have suffered. This is because the jurors will *hear* your objection as trying to hide something from them. And even though the basis for your objection—that is, the *truth*—might be that the evidence is not important enough to outweigh its prejudice, the jury will *perceive* the evidence to be important. Why else would your opponent be trying to get it in? So by failing to file a motion in limine, you widen the gap between what the jurors hear and what they perceive to be the truth.

Consider also the interplay between the four elements—(a) what you say; (b) what jurors hear; (c) what the truth is; and (d) what jurors perceive the truth to be. As I mentioned, the credibility gap is a function of the relationship between (b) and (d).

But there are other important relationships. For example, the difference between (a), what you say, and (c), what the truth is, is dependent on your objective honesty at trial. The more you embellish, the wider this particular gap—let's call it the "honesty gap"—gets. But if you've closed the credibility gap, then the honesty gap becomes less important for the purposes of the trial. Of course, sacrificing honesty for perceived credibility just to win a case is something that all too many lawyers make the mistake of doing.

Another example is the difference between (a), what you say, and (b), what jurors hear. This one is a function of how well you communicate, and we can call it the "comprehension gap." If your words tend to confuse the jury—perhaps because you failed to adequately prepare what you were going to say—then credibility becomes much less relevant. They may believe you, but confused jurors in the deliberation room may not be able to make the right decisions.

The ideal situation is to have all four elements close together on the continuum. This requires you to be clear, credible, and honest. Not surprisingly, the distance between each element grows exponentially. That is to say that once the jury believes that you are credible, they will tend to downplay minor missteps. But if the jury thinks that they can't believe anything you say, then even the smallest mistakes will seem enormous to them. What would be an inch of movement in the credibility gap becomes a mile if the jury believes that they can't trust you. And at some point, it becomes virtually impossible to close the gap and regain your credibility with the jury. This is the gist of the anonymous quotation at the beginning of this chapter. So as you read through this and the next few chapters, consider how each topic plays into the credibility gap.

2. Building Credibility and Using It in the Courtroom

More than 2,000 years ago, Aristotle penned *The Art of Rhetoric*, a book that even today is considered the cornerstone of rhetoric theory. In it, he says:

> [I]t is not only necessary to consider how to make the speech itself demonstrative and convincing, but also that the speaker should show himself to be of a certain character . . . and that his hearers should think that he is disposed in a certain way toward them; and further, that they themselves should be disposed in a certain way towards him.[1]

So for over two millennia, we have known and understood that effective persuasion has not only to do with what you say, but how you say it and what you look like when you do. And there are a number of techniques that will help improve your credibility throughout the trial.

Keep in mind, however, that not all of the techniques will work for each phase of trial. The manner in which you make your opening statement must necessarily differ from the manner in which you make your closing argument. Your credibility in opening depends solely on *you*, the speaker. But in closing, you have the benefit of the evidence and testimony you've put on, so your credibility depends both on *you* and *the people and things you're associated with*. Some people call this the difference between internal and external credibility, but I think it makes more sense to think of the difference as being between direct and indirect credibility.

You develop direct credibility during those times that you are presenting yourself to the jury. In voir dire and opening, for example, the

---

1. ARISTOTLE, THE ART OF RHETORIC 169 (J.H. Freese trans., Harvard University Press 1982).

spotlight is on you. But on direct examination of your witnesses, the spotlight is on them. If you put on the country's foremost expert on some issue relevant to your case, then you build your own credibility indirectly through their words and actions.

The other takeaway from the Aristotle passage above is that you have to *appear* to be credible. Your suit, your posture, your grooming are all factors that play into how believable you are. You should always make eye contact with each person you're speaking to. This doesn't mean just looking at them; wait until they are looking back at you before you say anything. That tells them that what you have to say is so important that you have to wait until you have their attention before you say it.

Also, remember to smile at the jurors. Smiling is one of the most powerful human connections we have. Smiling begins in early infancy, and is a critical factor in helping parents bond with a newborn. The rest of our lives, smiling factors into social bonding and enhances our likability. Smiling can help you influence people, even when it appears the odds are stacked against you. For example, studies indicate that a nice smile is one of our main criteria for electing presidents. It's such an important aspect of our body language that Allan and Barbara Pease dedicated an entire chapter of their book, *The Definitive Book of Body Language*, to describing the influence a smile has on others.

Your knowledge of the case and the underlying law also play into your credibility. Just as bringing the foremost expert in the country in on an issue improves your credibility, so too does *being* the foremost expert *on this case*. In Chapter 2, I mentioned that certain professionals have instant credibility just because of what they do. Just about every poll conducted on credibility shows that teachers and medical professionals have it, while lawyers and lobbyists don't. So don't be a lawyer at trial—be a teacher. Teach the jury the nuances of the case through testimony. When your opponent is wrong about something, don't just call him on it, but show your expertise by explaining why he was wrong. And always give the jury information in a way that they can relate to, given their knowledge and experience.

This last point is key. Speaking to the jury in legalese widens the comprehension gap—the gap between what you say and what they hear. Relating something to them in a way that hits home does the opposite. And the bonus is that you earn credibility by virtue of talking to the jury as a peer of theirs, one who identifies with them. Some of the most effective lawyers I've seen are effective because they pay attention to these sorts of details. They might share experiences with the jury, such as getting stuck in a traffic jam on the way to the courthouse or getting drenched because of the downpour. This simple technique of building a connection with the jurors is often lost on some lawyers, perhaps because they underestimate its effectiveness. So I urge you not to overlook these details.

3. Learning from the Master: Aristotle

We've all heard the military's formula for presenting a plan or idea: Tell them what you are going to say; say it; then tell them what you said. It may strike you as repetitive, but this is a valuable means of preparing for a trial.

However, there is a better model to be found in Aristotle's *Art of Rhetoric*, which effectively laid the groundwork for modern public communication in 350b.c.e. You are probably familiar with the Socrates-Plato-Aristotle connection. Socrates was Plato's teacher and Plato was Aristotle's. Throughout Plato's work, he depicts Socrates as engaging in conversations with various members of high society. The conversations start innocently enough, but as they proceed, Socrates unveils the flaws in his counterpart's argument, often shaking an entire belief system or at least exposing the person as a hypocrite.

So it was when Plato wrote about the Sophists, philosophers of his time who only catered to high society. The Sophists allegedly used dirty tricks in argumentation; they split hairs, talked in circles, and so on. Their goal was not to be right, but to win the argument. Plato's depiction of the Sophists as dishonest carried through time. Hence the term "sophistry."

But Aristotle saw the situation in a different light. He believed that rhetoric, or the art of orating, was worthy of deep study and analysis. More important, he believed that good rhetoric was both persuasive and ethical. In analyzing rhetoric, Aristotle realized that public speaking is always a mix of three of its aspects, which he called "proofs." The proofs are *ethos*, *pathos*, and *logos*. Let's continue our Aristotelian discussion by defining these central terms.[2]

---

2. Daniel Christensen, "Select the right jury for your case: here's how to root out bias among potential jurors during voir dire to strengthen your client's chance of a fair trial," *Trial*, April, 2004.

> Ethos is your personal credibility, the faith people have in your integrity. Ethos is the attraction to your presentation based on your character. Why should the audience listen to you speaking on this topic?

> Pathos is the speaker's ability to connect to the audience's feeling; it is the empathic side. Is the audience drawn into the presentation at an emotional level? Are you connecting with the audience at the heart level?

> Logos is the substance: the words, the organization, the logic. It is the appeal of your presentation based on reasoning. Is the presentation logical and well-supported?

In the pages that follow, we will examine techniques for using all three of these concepts in the courtroom. We'll delve into questions of pathos in Chapter 6, and a fuller discussion of logos will appear in Chapter 7.

4. Ethos: Credibility Through Appearance

Remember the maxim that you never get a second chance to make a first impression? This statement does not simply point out the obvious. Rather, it implies that there is some value to making a good first impression. Of course, we all know this. The question is how to make use of this concept in the courtroom and with the jury.

In a trial setting, first impressions count, because they define the starting point for managing the credibility gap. Although most people distrust lawyers, I've come to realize that it's a distrust of the profession, not of individuals. So although you might think that the credibility gap is already set by common distrust of lawyers, I find the opposite to be the case. Certainly, some people come into voir dire expecting to be lied to. But for the most part, people start off trusting that the lawyer is being honest in voir dire. Perhaps this is because the judge is in the room, or because the first few statements you make can't help but be true (for example, telling the jury it's important whether any of them knows any of the parties is patently true and the jurors recognize that). But what you say does make a difference. If you are anything but honest and sincere in your voir dire, then you run the risk of widening the gap. And remember, each new misstep broadens the gap exponentially more than the last.

So the first few words at trial help you build your ethos—your character and appearance. Here you are given the opportunity to establish yourself as both the expert and the teacher. Is anyone likely to listen to a dissertation on ethics from Bernie Madoff? At trial, you can't just say, "I'm credible and a good trial lawyer so you must listen to me." The jury would laugh at you as a clown or ignore you as just another arrogant lawyer. Instead, as trial lawyers, we must earn credibility because our actions and words convey experience and credibility.

Your goal in the courtroom is to employ words, movements, and actions that radiate confidence and trustworthiness. If you're confident and earn the jury's trust, you'll also hold their attention as you present evidence and themes.

In this section, I'll share with you my formula for personal credibility. Though I have no formal training in psychology, I'm a lifelong student of people and human nature. I've always been fascinated by how we appreciate and respond to different situations and people. Based on my own personal observation and experience, some patterns seem clear: As a general rule, we follow advice and direction of those we perceive to be experts or authority figures. In my experience, credible people look the part, speak with enthusiasm, exude relaxed confidence, feel comfortable in their own skin, and master their subject matter.

It's a fact that how people perceive you makes a difference in how you're treated. Observing mock trials over the years, I'm always amazed by how quickly a foreperson is selected. At most, the process takes about two minutes and the decision is made based on little if any substantive information about the person selected. How do jurors come to this decision so quickly? Quite frankly, it's a fairly superficial decision-making process. I want to emphasize that jurors are not superficial. In fact, in my experience, the contrary is true: juries work very hard to get the right answer. But the election of a foreperson is more a reflection of society's definition of power and success than a deliberative process. Forepersons tend to be higher-status white males and are often college educated. Many have had prior jury experience. Their behavior, speech, and appearance (dress such as collared shirt, sport coat, or suit and paraphernalia such as briefcase or computer bag) signal to fellow jurors that they are, at least in society's currency, higher-status people. During mock trials, they'll often walk in and assume the position at the head of the table and be the first to remind the group of the need to elect a foreperson. In short, they are your leaders and authority figures.

The jury room is not the only place this holds true. The jury room is merely a microcosm of society as a whole. Any sociologist will tell you that when you dress well, you'll receive better treatment. The world around us is full of empirical evidence of this truism. When you dress well, you'll get better service from waitstaff. When you're traveling, you'll get better upgrades for hotel rooms or rental vehicles. People assume that those who dress well have a greater status and greater social standing, and will act more appropriately than someone who dresses casually and doesn't pay attention to grooming. Don't take my word for it. Test this for yourself. Go to a mall where you can sit in front of a business that has a wall of windows where you can easily see inside. Take note of the salespeople or waitstaff there. When they interact with a customer, see if there's a difference in their behavior toward the customer who's wearing a jogging suit and toward a customer who's professionally dressed in a business suit. You'll be amazed at the difference. Dressing well gives you instant credibility. It's a fact of human nature.

The courtroom dictates that your dress will be professional. For instance, if you were to wear khakis and a polo shirt, the judge would probably throw you out—but if she did not, the jury would be confused as to your role given your casual dress. As courtroom lawyers, we have to abide by a certain dress code. It's simple: dress professionally (not ostentatiously, but professionally) all the time. Does this mean that every business day you have to wear a suit? To me, yes, but for a different reason. I want clients to see me in the exact same light as a jury. Because I meet with clients daily and never know when a new client might want to meet to discuss a new case, I'm always prepared and wear a suit every weekday at the office. Many firms, including my own (over my dissenting vote), have adopted a casual dress policy in some format or another. I'm widely ridiculed because I will not observe them. My basic reason is essentially the same: I want my clients to think of me as a trial lawyer. Trial lawyers wear suits to court. You'll never convince me that khakis and an open-collar polo convey that hard-edged confidence that a client is looking for in a trial lawyer. Do you have to adopt my policy and constantly go around in a suit and a tie to everything you attend in your day-to-day profession? No, but I would do it when you want people to think of you as a trial lawyer. This is just a suggestion at your disposal that you can use to your advantage for your business. Be your own advertising whenever you go out. You never know who you might run into: potential clients, current clients, opposing counsel, or judges.

Remember, attention to the details of your appearance matters. Plan for the physical impression you will make in the courtroom. Think carefully about the message your attire and overall appearance will convey to the jury. Will you wear a nice, simple tie that exudes confidence and class? Or will you put on a tie that your child gave you last Christmas . . . golf balls and all? There is a time and place for everything, but in your profession, you want to be taken seriously. Do your best not to appear "invisible" when presenting your case. For example, if you are lead counsel, but you need associates in the courtroom with you, make sure they all wear the same colored suit and that your suit color is different. If you are on the same level as your cocounsel, then all of you should wear different suits. Think back to the O.J. Simpson trial—do you remember F. Lee Bailey, Robert Shapiro, Alan Dershowitz, and Johnnie Cochran ever wearing the same colored suit? Do you think that was a coincidence?

The point is that you don't want to stand out inappropriately, but you also don't want to hide from the jury. Lecterns and tables are your enemies at trial. If the court's rules allow it, stand in front of the table, not behind it. When you stand behind a desk or a table, the jury only sees your upper body. Many lawyers feel protected and safe behind the lectern. They look down at their notes and keep their hands gripped to the edge of the podium. This is a critical mistake and sends a message of insecurity or even hostility toward the opposing side in cases where emotions run high.

Think of it this way: Trial work is the opposite of golf. In golf, it's essential to keep your head down to make good contact with the ball. In trial work, it's essential to keep your head up to make good contact with your jury. If you want to own the courtroom, people need to see you from head to toe. Step out from behind the lectern, desk, or table and you'll project a stronger message.

Your posture will also help you appear more credible. All those years of your mother telling you to sit up straight have finally paid off. The jury doesn't want to see you slouching in your seat or leaning against the podium with all your weight on one leg. You exude confidence and credibility when you stand tall and sit up straight. It may seem uncomfortable at first, especially if you're not used to it. But you should always sacrifice comfort to avoid looking sloppy.

Keep in mind that credibility lies deeper than your physical presentation. It's in your spirit. People are drawn to others who are comfortable in their own skin. Are you dissatisfied with your looks? Get over it. That's not what audiences truly care about. If people sense that you're trying too hard to impress them, your behavior waves a red flag of insecurity. Your overblown efforts make them wonder what you're trying to hide or compensate for. Remember what Shakespeare wrote in *Hamlet*: "The lady doth protest too much. . . ."

An active and energetic trial lawyer can gain the attention of almost any jury. When you rise to speak, the jury models its response on your behavior. Audiences, whether at a play or a trial, generally want he who struts and frets his hour upon the stage to succeed. They want you to engage and entertain them. Most people are starving for something interesting to occupy their minds. If people are not starved for entertainment, how do you explain the high ratings for reality TV? Be enthusiastic about your client, about your case, and about the opportunity to be actually trying a case, and the jury will appreciate that you believe what you're telling them and that it must be important.

Ms. Wynn, my high school geometry teacher, was so enthusiastic about geometry that even this teenage jock was interested and entertained in class. My friends from other classes complained bitterly that geometry was awful and boring, while my classmates and I actually enjoyed the challenge and looked forward to her class. The evidence was pretty clear that the material alone was not compelling. Ms. Wynn had the same curriculum as every other geometry teacher at Captain Shreve High School. What made the difference was her genuine passion and enthusiasm for teaching. When you stand up to present your opening, be enthusiastic. You can't be acting or pretending. It must be genuine. If it is, people will be drawn to you, and to what you have to say.

Jurors, like any audience, sense when you're scared or self-conscious. If you give any indication that you're insecure, they'll lose interest fast. On the other hand, people are naturally drawn to those who show confidence. Notice I said "show confidence." Simply being confident is not enough. It doesn't do much good if you confidently stand in the corner. Credible advocates embody confidence by the way they stand, the way they speak, and the things they say.

One technique to appear more confident is to speak and move slowly. Most people rush when they speak. I know I did at first. In my first trial, the court reporter nicknamed me The Silver Bullet. Unfortunately, it wasn't because I rode the white horse, but because I spoke so fast. In my experience, successful people take their time. They give weight to their words. Did you ever see Ronald Reagan—who still today is remembered as The Great Communicator—speed through a speech? Do you think that Abraham Lincoln delivered the Gettysburg Address in a rapid-fire staccato cadence? No, and I doubt it. Making yourself slow down and taking your time will actually hold attention, because the jurors will perceive that you must be saying something important. They will feel drawn to listen to you. When you talk more slowly, people will wait for you, and then you can control the pace of your encounter with them.

When I first started trying cases, I thought if I raced through my words and thoughts, a quick delivery would reach the jury before their attention wandered. Let me tell you that that is a sure-fire method to lose their attention, and it's the way I learned about the concept I now call Juror Overload. People can accept only a certain amount of new information each minute. When you overload them, jurors take in even less than they are normally capable of taking in. Remember: for you, your case is familiar; for them, it's new. Your mind glosses over the information you already know and easily selects words that are familiar to you. Your familiarity becomes a problem if it causes you to move rapidly through the basic information. Your jury, however, is being exposed to you, your case, your facts, and your themes for the first time. Their brains need extra time to process and organize the new information. Help them by speaking and even moving slower than you normally do. Give other people time to let your information sink in.

He who keeps the other person waiting is in control. We have all had the experience of waiting at the doctor's office. I have and it drives me crazy. The person who causes the wait builds anticipation about the meeting within the mind of the person kept waiting. However, used in small doses—say, a three- or five-second pause—it can be used to gather focus and attention. Every great speaker pauses at the start to gather attention and tension. While they wait, people become hungry for you to start and eager to listen. If you examine the behavior of people who work for a billionaire (and I have been around a few of Texas's finest), they usually act very rapidly, like worker bees serving the queen bee. The queen stays in the hive, while the workers buzz here and flit there. The billionaire watches his staff hop, jump, and scurry while he sits and waits for results. He doesn't need to move quickly, because he has other people who will do this for him. When you stand before the jury to speak, you control the pace by how fast you speak or ask questions.

This is a lesson we can learn from the sales world. Have you ever heard the saying "He who speaks first loses"? One of the reasons for this primary rule of sales is to allow your proposal to sink into the prospective customer's mind. Let them mull it around and consider it. By speaking before they've had time to process the offer, you could lose the sale. When applying this to the courtroom, it's not too different. Of course you're going to be the first to speak, but you have to allow your important statements to linger or hang a little before re-engaging the jury and moving on to something else that the juror must process. Remember to maintain control by pausing before you begin, and again to punctuate important points or questions.

In normal conversation, people split their attention. Half is on what you are saying, and half is on what they will say next. This is an unfortunate truth in our fast-paced society. One of the best techniques to capture people's full attention is silence. In theatre, this is called the "dramatic pause." After you make an important point or before you ask an important question, stop. Don't rush from one point to the next. Let your message sink in or give the jury a chance to refocus their attention before you make an especially important point. Remind yourself to stop after you've said something important. Silence creates texture in your presentations. The absence of sound draws people in and focuses their attention.

Also, stand up when you speak in a courtroom. Always. Standing draws the jury's attention to you. Standing and moving often enables you to project more energy in your voice. Standing also tends to cause the speaker to be more concise. Studies show that people gain credibility, persuasive power, and stature when they stand.[3] Standing has also been shown to increase the speaker's reaction time.

---

3. Allan and Barbara Pease, *The Definitive Book of Body Language,* 363 (2004).

A 1998 study done at University of Southern California found that "individuals' information-processing speed accelerates 5% to 20% for several tasks that involve rapid decision making when they are standing as compared with when they're sitting."[4]

In short, standing or moving stimulates brain centers associated with reactive capacity, so you react faster. In the experiment, subjects were asked to stand or sit before a computer monitor that registered their response times to various requests. Subjects responded faster when standing. The takeaway is, if you want to increase your authority, draw attention, and be "mentally" quicker on your feet, then get up out of that chair and move around.

Contrary to intuition, the majority of a speaker's impact comes through nonverbal communication. A famous series of studies by UCLA psychology professor Albert Mehrabian demonstrated that face-to-face communication relies on three elements: words, tone of voice, and body language. Specifically, Professor Mehrabian's study found that when it comes to communication about attitudes or emotions, listeners unconsciously weigh factors differently in determining a speaker's believability. The cues they rely on are:

> Visual: 55 percent (body language, eye contact, gestures)
> Vocal: 38 percent (voice, volume, cadence)
> Verbal: 7 percent (words)

In the movie *Hitch*, Will Smith captured the results of the Mehrabian study in his advice on dating: "90% of what you're saying ain't coming out of your mouth."[5]

So how does this play out in the courtroom? Think of it in terms of the credibility gap. To you, what you say might encompass all you want the jury to hear. But what they hear is also colored by your attire, grooming, posture, etc. In effect, what they hear is determined in large part by your ethos. So when there's a conflict between what you say and the rest of the message you're conveying, the jury will weigh your appearance and gestures more than your words. This in turn, will widen the credibility gap.

4. http://college.use.edu/labs/dawson/documents/Attentionalstagesofinformationprocess.pdf.
5. Finest Quotes, http://www.finestquotes.com/movie_quotes/movie/Hitch/page/0.htm (last visited Mar. 13, 2011).

Thus your nonverbal communications can reinforce your words, or they can detract from them. A famous story in Texas helps to highlight this point. It is about an East Texas criminal defense lawyer whose client was on trial for murder. In his closing, to demonstrate the point of reasonable doubt, he dramatically pointed to the door and told the jury that the real murderer was about to walk in the courtroom. Seeing that everyone on the jury jerked their head to the entrance of the courtroom, the criminal defense lawyer knew he had created the reasonable doubt necessary to gain an acquittal for his client. He was shocked to learn that after a brief 30-minute deliberation, the jury returned a guilty verdict against his client. In an interview with a juror after the trial, the lawyer asked, "How did you convict him? When I said the murderer was about to walk in the courtroom, the entire jury turned to watch the door." The juror smiled and responded, "Yes, we all turned our heads, but your client didn't even move."

Nonverbal communication is called the "silent language." Always remember that your credibility is harmed when you send conflicting messages. And just as your body language should match your words, so too should your client's body language. To the best of your ability, convince your client that his body language is just as important as yours. And if you ever plan a stunt like the one in the example above, make sure you consider how it's going to play into your ethos.

CHAPTER 6

What Trial Lawyers Learn from Actors

> "Life is like a play; it's not the length but the
> excellence of the acting that matters."
>
> —*Seneca*

Audiences (whether jury members, sports fans, or concertgoers) value and appreciate skill. A display of skill confirms to onlookers that you're capable of delivering on the promises of proof you make in the opening. For example, I know little about gymnastics, other than that my seven-year-old daughter is in the Tumblers Level 2 class at the local YMCA. However, I'm in awe when I witness an Olympic gymnast give a masterful performance. I value and appreciate the medal-winning gymnasts, because I can imagine how long and hard they must have trained. Upon witnessing greatness, people often feel inspired. They're reminded that human potential is limitless.

How does this translate in the courtroom? If you have skill, use it, but don't flaunt it (especially when facing a less experienced or competent adversary). Keep your ego in check. Never show off simply to make yourself look good. Nothing turns off an audience more quickly than a hotshot.

First, be technically proficient at what a trial lawyer does. Either pre-admit your exhibits or know how to admit exhibits. Don't fumble over your words or look lost and confused when hit with an evidentiary objection. Anticipate evidentiary issues, be prepared with the right hearsay exception, and especially know the business records requirements cold.

Second, know your case inside and out. You must have complete mastery of time lines, names, dates, and exhibit numbers. Without explicitly telling people, you demonstrate that you're the master of your case. Showing beats telling every time. Persuasion is your main concern when speaking before a jury, so you have to know what you're talking about. Your goal is to compel the jury to accept your case by eliciting facts, demonstrating truths, and supporting your themes.

Third, be an expert on the law. This means more than the law of evidence or procedure. Be an expert on the substantive law of your case. Sure, you're in front of the jury because nobody knows the facts of your case better than you. But your client likely hired you because of your experience in this area of law. When you deliver your closing argument, you are going to have to translate the technical jargon of whatever law you're dealing with into plain English. Then you're going to have to explain to the jury how your facts fit within that law. If you only have a general understanding of the law that pertains to your case, your arguments will barely make sense. If the jury thinks that you have a command of the law, even if they don't understand it, they will be more likely to believe you when you talk about it.

We've all seen politicians, journalists, and even lawyers who wow us with their ability to speak in public when their speech is prepared. But some of those people cannot intelligently answer a single follow-up question on the very same topic that they just delivered an entire speech about. When you see this, you know that the speaker, whoever it may be, is simply not that well-versed in topic. The speaker loses credibility, and you almost want to yell at him for wasting your time while he stumbles over his own words trying to come up with an answer.

I've watched this scene play out repeatedly in the courtroom. An unprepared attorney shuffles through stacks of papers while searching for evidence that was not presented to the court ahead of the trial. Jurors shift anxiously in their chairs. The judge exhales deeply, unimpressed by the waste of time. And the attorney's image as a professional diminishes within seconds. Preparation is one of the most important aspects of presenting a case.

Before you step in front of the jury, ask yourself, "Why am I here?" I learned this from a friend of mine who is an actor. The best entertainers know the answer to this question: "I'm here for the audience." The same is true in the courtroom. The jury doesn't exist to satisfy you. Rather, you exist to inform and educate the jury. The fact is that the jury cares about one thing, which is their personal experience in the courtroom. It's the job of the trial lawyer to focus on that experience and make sure it's efficient and informative. Love your jury. Before you rise to speak to the jury, tell yourself, "I love my jury, I love my jury. . . ." The jury will feel this and recognize the connection. You'll also prime yourself for a positive experience.

Shakespeare wrote, "All the world's a stage, and all the men and women merely players." You may never step onto a real stage, but you can use the techniques you learn in this book to make your trial presentations more dramatic and more effective. The nuts-and-bolts techniques in this book will help you on your way to becoming a real showperson, which is certainly something to aspire to. This is a lesson that I learned from my partner, Jeff Tillotson. In a trial in federal court, Jeff and I were defending a manufacturer of circuit boards in a contracts case. The plaintiff alleged that our client had failed to deliver quality product. On the direct examination of their project manager, our opponents had spent a significant amount of time discussing one particular letter complaining that a delivery of circuit boards had been late. This was not what the case was about, but it was not a particularly good fact for us. On cross-examination, Jeff used a subsequent letter to show that the particular circuit boards, though delivered late, were accepted without complaint. To make his point clear, he found a copy of the much-discussed letter from direct examination and said, "So all of the complaints in this letter were addressed and resolved?" When the witness agreed, Jeff loudly ripped the document and asked, "So this document is completely worthless in helping this jury resolve this case?" That is beautiful showmanship. He made the evidentiary point that the exhibit had no value and, even more importantly, he assaulted the credibility of our adversary by proving that he had tried to trick the jury and wasted their time.

When you are a showperson, people will inch forward in their seats to hear what you have to say. Their attention won't leave you, because they don't want to miss what you might say or do next. Have you been to the circus lately? The ringmaster for the circus speaks with lively language, walks with a confident gait, and delivers material with a twinkle in his eye. You can become a courtroom master by attending to the details outlined in this chapter and throughout the book. And the best way to learn is to actually get in front of juries and see what they respond to best. The more you use these techniques, the more they will become your own. It's been said that after 21 days of repeating something, it becomes habit, so practice your delivery in front of a mirror before stepping into a courtroom. After a while, you won't even have to think about your technique or delivery, because, like riding a bike, it will become second nature.

In this chapter, I will give you some of the best tools for connecting with the jury. Remember that public speaking is about making an impact on your audience. To do this, you need to get their attention, meet their needs while you have their attention, and be clear in your method of communication. The ultimate goal is to make a connection with the jury, to create a bond with them that makes it difficult for them to return a verdict for your opponent.

1. Remain Cool, Calm, and Confident

Before going into the discussion on building connections with the jury, I think it is important to discuss nervousness. All lawyers, even the best ones, experience the jitters. I know a lawyer who has an uncanny ability to appear calm and cool in court. It's almost as if his mother delivered him right there in the well of the courtroom. So I was shocked to hear him admit that before a trial begins he feels sick to the point of throwing up. He told me that he argued a case in front of the United States Supreme Court, but that he almost missed the docket call because he was in the bathroom trying to collect himself. Nervousness is a human trait, and we are all affected by it. Although you may never eliminate it, you can reduce it, sometimes so much that it's insignificant.

To understand how nerves affect the jury, consider three hypothetical situations. The first is an attorney who isn't nervous at all. She appears completely confident in everything she does and says, and the whole process seems comfortable to her. Here, the jury will not even think about how nerve-racking the process actually is. This leaves the attorney free to make a strong connection with the jury.

The second hypothetical attorney is only slightly nervous. Her voice shakes, her forehead glistens with sweat, and she seems a little uncomfortable. For her, making a connection with the jury actually begins with the nervousness. In other words, she can get the jury to identify with her nervousness because they imagine what it would be like to be on the spot. The problem here is that her nerves are actually detracting from her message. So even if the audience connects with her, their attention is drawn away from her case and to her demeanor. This situation is not ideal, but it's better than the next.

The third hypothetical attorney's nervousness is debilitating. She can hardly get a sentence out; she is sweating through her blouse and fumbling with her papers. Here, the jury ignores her words and case altogether because the only thing they can concentrate on is the attorney's performance. In time, their confidence is lost—they start to wonder why she is even here, and why their time is being wasted. Even if they identify with her somewhat, her message is lost on the jury.

So how do you get rid of your nerves? This is probably the single hardest question to answer in this book. There is no one-size-fits-all solution. Some people say to picture everyone in the room naked. To me, that sounds a little silly. Have you ever been the only dressed person in a room full of naked people? Me neither, but I can't imagine that it would make me less nervous. Quite the opposite—we get nervous when we're the center of attention, and what could be more attention-grabbing than being the only one who's different? But some people swear by this technique, and if it works for them, then so be it.

There are, however, some techniques that have almost garnered a consensus on how to reduce nervousness. They are: acting the part, being overprepared, and, as will be the focus in the second half of this chapter, connecting with the jury.

There's no question that your mind is a powerful weapon. It can play tricks on you and make you believe something that's not true. So if you're overly nervous about your presentation, then one way to reduce your nerves is to trick yourself into thinking that you're not you. That is, you can act the part of the confident lawyer: fake it till you make it. You can do this in two ways—you can manipulate either the physical or psychological aspects of your presentation. As you practice these techniques, you'll come to find that the former is much easier than the latter.

As to the physical, you can train yourself to project an appearance of being confident even when you're not. For example, practice walking around with good posture. Hold your head high and control your breathing. If you're shaking uncontrollably, focus on something else. You can also shift the jury's focus to something else or someone else. The best time to do this is on direct examination. Remember that on direct, the main attraction is the witness. You are just a sideshow, and your only job is to facilitate the witness's testimony. Of course, the focus will shift to you if you ask objectionable questions, so prepare your questions in advance and consider running them by another attorney. You'll do wonders for your nerves if you can get through one direct without the jury ever looking at you. If you know that you have a nervous tic that you can't get rid of, try to turn it around into your favor.

A good example of someone who used his nerves to his advantage was Elvis. On his first stage appearance he was so nervous that his leg began to shake. That nervous shake propelled him into the hearts of millions of fans and became the trademark of his stage presence. The audience loved it! This is proof that sometimes a flaw can turn into an asset.

Manipulating your own psyche is much harder. You basically have to lie to yourself and you have to believe your own lie. But with practice, this technique actually works. Begin by going to the courthouse and watching a day or two of trial. Pick out your favorite attorney and take notes on his or her mannerisms, demeanor, and even attire. You can also mix and match between styles—if you like something one lawyer does and something else that another lawyer does, combine them. You can also look to legal television shows or movies for inspiration. At the end of the day, you should have an "ideal lawyer" in mind. Then "game film" certain hypotheticals with your ideal lawyer. Literally, roll the film in your mind: How would this lawyer react to an objection? How would this lawyer impeach a witness? Would he or she give an emotional closing argument or a logical one? The last step, of course, is to incorporate your ideal lawyer's behavior into your own. In your preparation for trial, don't draft questions that you would ask; draft questions that he or she would ask. If you're taken by surprise at trial—for example, by an objection you didn't anticipate or a witness who turns hostile—take a moment to think about how your ideal lawyer would react. The more preparation you get (whether live or through "game filming" your ideal lawyer), the more adept you will become in the courtroom. And before long, you'll realize that you *are* your ideal lawyer!

The second way of calming your nerves is to be overly prepared for trial. You should know your facts inside and out. Rehearse your entire opening statement and practice it until it has become second nature. Of course, you can have notes, but reduce them to keywords, reminders, and signposts only to be referred to if you've lost your place. As to your witnesses, you should spend as much time as you can prior to trial going over their testimony. You should know exactly what your witness is going to say, anticipate what objections the testimony might draw, and know how to respond to them ahead of time. Also practice getting physical evidence in. Different types of physical evidence require different foundational facts before they are admissible. You should be ready to lay the groundwork for every piece of evidence, and you should know the proper response to every objection your opponent may raise. If you've practiced the entire trial, your muscle memory will take over and your nerves won't even have the opportunity to get in the way.

These points about preparation always remind me of the movie *My Cousin Vinny*. Joe Pesci played the part of a New York attorney who, having finally passed the bar just weeks before, stepped into court for the first time to defend his cousin wrongfully accused of murder while traveling through a small Alabama town. After numerous disappointments and misunderstandings during which Pesci was held in contempt of court and incarcerated overnight, one of the defendants decided to use the court-appointed attorney. Compared to Pesci, this attorney seemed to have it all: experience, knowledge, and a suit. (Pesci offended the judge with his leather jacket and casual style). While Pesci dozed off at trial, the more experienced defense attorney addressed the jury. To the surprise of all, he was barely able to utter a word without stuttering. His explanation? Nerves. Although Pesci lacked experience or knowledge of courtroom procedures, he won the hearts and minds of everyone because in the end he found confidence in his abilities. His confidence carried him through his first trial and on to victory. So relax and find confidence in your abilities, even if you're new to the courtroom.

The last way to reduce your level of nervousness is to connect with the jury. Imagine sitting at your family's dinner table, telling them a story. Have you ever been nervous talking in front of them? If not, the reason is because you know your audience well. You have a connection with them and you realize that you have nothing to prove to them. They already know you and their perception of your credibility will not change based on this one story. In a trial, however, this assurance isn't there. You don't have that same familial comfort with your audience, so you worry about their perceptions of you. And the more you worry, the more nervous you get.

This is why you work to build a connection with your audience early. Once you have made that connection, you will be more comfortable speaking in front of them. They will no longer be strangers, but rather a group of friends in whom you can confide. And once you've broken down this barrier, you will be more comfortable presenting your case to them. The next section will stress the importance of building empathy with the jury, and creating a connection with them. Creating this connection is what Aristotle called *pathos*.

2. Pathos: Building Empathy

In the previous chapter, we discussed *ethos*, the art of persuading your audience based on your moral character. To persuade jurors using ethos, you have to show them that you are a credible source of information, that they can rely on what you say because you are inherently trustworthy. But ethos was only the beginning. Aristotle's second mode of persuasion is *pathos*, an appeal to the audience's emotions. In this section, we will discuss how to persuade the jury by getting them to *empathize* with you, your client, and your case.

Notice that I did not say *sympathize* with you. There is a difference between sympathy and empathy, but the two terms are often confused for each other. Sympathy is an appreciation for someone's feelings, while empathy a shared feeling through a common experience. For example, if your boss is upset one day because her dog passed away, you might sympathize with her, even if you have never had a dog. You can imagine her pain. On the other hand, if you owned a dog together and it passed away, you would empathize with her. You feel the same pain she feels.

Although subtle, the difference can mean a win or loss at trial. Getting the jury to sympathize with your case is a good first step. But even if the jury feels pity for your client's injuries, they might still return a verdict against you because they believe that the law favors your opponent or that he has the better argument. But once you get the jury to *empathize* with your client, it becomes tremendously more difficult for them to rule against you.

One of the best illustrations of this that I've seen was in the movie *A Time to Kill*. The movie is about a black man, played by Samuel L. Jackson, on trial for murdering two white men who beat and raped his 10-year-old daughter. Jackson's attorney, played by Matthew McConaughey, is faced with an extremely tough trial. It is the Deep South, the jury is all white, there were dozens of witnesses to the killings, and the judge seems to be denying all of his motions. In his closing argument, however, McConaughey wins the jury over with a compelling appeal to their emotions. He begins by apologizing for his missteps at trial, then goes on to describe at length the gory details of the rape of Jackson's daughter. At this point, we, the audience, understand that the jury merely sympathizes with Jackson and his daughter, but that they already knew all of these details and were still ready to convict. That is, until the end of his argument. After five minutes of describing the plight of the little girl, McConaughey says, "Now imagine she's white." With those four words, he turned sympathy into empathy and a conviction into an acquittal.

Now, it's hard for lawyers to watch movies about lawyers without becoming a tad cynical. Even though I don't practice criminal law, the lawyer in me wanted to stand up and object to the entire closing argument for confusing the issues, being irrelevant, and describing facts that are not in evidence. Despite being objectionable, however, the argument serves as a great example here for two reasons. First, it shows how powerful an emotional appeal can be. Until the end of McConaughey's closing argument, the facts about the little girl had not hit home for many of the jurors. The point is that sympathy alone may not win you the case. Second, it shows how important it is to be honest with the jury. It was crucial for McConaughey to rehabilitate his credibility before going into the meat of his argument because, otherwise, the jury might recognize that he was clouding the issues. So how do you master *pathos*? You begin by knowing what it is about your client that the jury will identify with. This involves two steps. First, you have to know your client almost as well as you know yourself. Does he have children? Is he a member of any community organizations? If your client is an organization, does it employ a lot of people in the community? Is it a small business? Does it donate to charities? You need this information because your goal is to get the jury to identify with your client. In other words, you want them to be able to empathize with your case.

Second, you have to know your audience. Obviously, voir dire is your best opportunity to get to know the jurors. Listen to their answers, but don't focus just on what they say, but how they say it. Try to glean from their answers how they feel about a certain subject. Also, consider using the Internet to determine which venire members would make the best jurors. A recent *Wall Street Journal* article discussed a major trend of lawyers bringing laptops and iPads into voir dire in order to look up potential jurors on social networking sites. Your initial reaction to this may be negative, but look at it this way—what people post about themselves on social media websites such as Facebook is information that you can get by asking direct questions in voir dire. Looking it up on the Internet is just a way to get the same information in a fraction of the time. It allows you to focus on more in-depth questions.

But regardless of how you conduct voir dire, don't limit learning about the jury to just that phase of the trial. While you present your case, you should be trying to get a sense for how the jury reacts to certain arguments, testimony, and evidence. The more you learn about the jurors throughout the trial, the more effective your closing argument can be.

A word of warning—there is a general courtroom rule that says that you cannot ask the jury to put themselves in your client's shoes. For instance, you can't say to the jury, "If you lost an arm in a tractor, like my client did, how much would you want to be awarded? Then that's how much you should award my client." This is called a "Golden Rule" argument, and the reason courts don't allow it is because it encourages a jury to depart from its role as a neutral fact-finder. At first blush, it may seem that by appealing to pathos, you're violating this rule. But keep in mind that there's a difference between explicitly asking the jury to put themselves in your client's shoes and subtly persuading them to empathize with your client.

As I mentioned above, finding the common denominator between your client and the jury is only the first step. You actually have to connect the two. You do this by focusing on the jury. After all, they're the reason you're speaking. Your efforts will be in vain and your client's case lost if you can't bring them to your point of view. You have to create a link between you and your jury to win your case. This is a concept I will continually repeat because it's one of the most important ingredients in my recipe for success. This connection can be made through personal anecdotes, humor, or even something as simple as a smile. The goal is to create feelings between you and your jury so they believe what you say is true, important, and well worth their attention. This will result in a smooth flow for the duration of the trial and is possibly the key to persuasion. Why? They will pay attention and listen to your ideas.

I've talked to many lawyers who say that they don't know how well they are connecting with their juries, if at all. The best technique I've found to cure this is to speak to one juror at a time. During opening or closing, I look directly at one juror as I make a point. Of course, I don't focus on just one juror the entire time. And I don't focus on the juror who was my favorite during voir dire or the one who smiles each time I look at her. I give one juror my undivided attention as I make point one, and then I give another juror my undivided attention as I make my next point, and so on throughout my argument. I use this one-juror-at-a-time technique because looking someone in the eye forces me to speak in an engaging manner.

Looking at one juror at a time is more of a technical tool to connect with the jury. Other obvious ones include your posture and your tone of voice, both of which we discussed in Chapter 5. If you maintain a good posture and a positive attitude throughout the trial, you will exude confidence and a winning mind-set. This, in turn, will make the jury want to be on your team. Let's face it—everyone likes to be around winners. As for your tone of voice, it is important to modulate it based on what you're talking about. If you're telling a sad story or questioning a victim, then your tone of voice should be calm and measured.

Another technical tool is clarity. In the courtroom, make statements that are clear and correct. Strive to stay away from statements that would confuse the jury in order to make your client look less guilty or culpable. At best, this will weaken the connection between you and the jury, weakening your persuasiveness through pathos. At worst, this will make you appear deceptive, weakening your persuasiveness through ethos. So when preparing your opening, for example, read it aloud and determine whether your words and thoughts are clear. If you can't tell, have someone listen to you as you read it out loud.

In addition to these technical tools, there are a number of stylistic tools that will help you connect with the jury. One of the best of these is the use of metaphors. Metaphors are tools we use to describe something in relation to another thing. They serve many purposes, but one of the main purposes is to aid in understanding a complex idea through a common experience or shared value. Our profession is already replete with metaphors. For example, we say that the First Amendment creates a *wall* of separation between the church and state, that a state can exercise personal jurisdiction over a nonresident through its *long-arm* statutes, and that the equity holders of a corporation can be personally liable by *piercing* the corporate *veil*. In fact, we use a metaphor to describe the law itself—justice is *blind*.

Metaphors are effective for connecting with the jury because they work on two levels. At the top level, the jury understands the message you are trying to convey, and appreciates the fact that you're trying to convey it in a way that makes sense to them. But at a deeper level, a metaphor highlights the fact that you share a common experience with a jury. A friend of mine is a master of using metaphors in trial. In a recent case, he was defending a wrongful termination suit, and one of his key goals at trial was to show that the plaintiff advanced through the company by taking credit for other people's work. So in his closing argument he said that the plaintiff "didn't climb the corporate ladder, but rather rode the corporate escalator." Notice that this statement would make no sense if his jury had never ridden an escalator before. I have since forgotten everything else about the case, but that one line just stuck with me. That, incidentally, was the point.

Another way to connect with the jury is through humor. When you're able to make the audience laugh in an otherwise boring case, they will love you for it. But remember that humor is not always effective, or even appropriate. In fact, if you have to ask yourself whether humor is appropriate in a certain trial, it's not. Factors that you should consider before cracking your first joke include the type of case, the type of client, and the type of humor. Obviously, there is almost no room for humor of any kind in certain criminal cases (e.g., murder, rape). Likewise, you should never use harsh or disparaging humor, especially pertaining to the people in the courtroom. This will make you look like a jerk and alienate the jury.

When I use humor, there is almost always a purpose beyond simply trying to make the jury like me. For example, I was giving a presentation on effective cross-examination and early on had problems with my clicker properly advancing the slide. I made fun of myself and the situation by saying, "Rule No. 1 is always practice with your equipment before you start a presentation." The audience laughed and I got things back on track. Here, I simply signaled to the audience that I was sensitive to the fact that this was an inconvenience for them, which strengthened our connection.

Finally, I would point out that honesty and sincerity are probably the most powerful tools for connecting with the audience. Some of the most powerful presenters are people who speak from the heart. When people sense that a message is communicated from the heart, they tend to believe it more strongly. A jury will quickly sense the difference between a lawyer who is genuine and one who is artificial. Some trial attorneys make the mistake of rehearsing their presentations to the point of over rehearsal—to the point that jurors find them to be phony or insincere. Don't just talk the talk. You must walk the walk. Are you passionate about your client's case? Then let the jury hear your passion. Put some feeling into your presentation.[1]

In a recent trial, I made a mistake in representing that a document evidenced that the defendant had bounced a check. I had done so because I honestly misread the document. I thought the document said that the defendant had bounced a check. The fact was important because one of the main issues in trial was how much cash the company had in the bank on a certain day. The defendant's witness pointed out in his examination that the check was not in fact a check bounced by the company. He pointed to a single small line on the document that said "deposit" and explained instead that a check written to the company had bounced. I knew that hurt my credibility, but in the heat of battle, I made a split-second decision to respond to the revelation of my error by going on the offensive on other points rather than apologize for what all now saw as a clear mistake. As I look back on that trial, I made the wrong decision. By not addressing my mistake I left the jury thinking I was trying to pull something over on them and surrendered a good portion of my personal credibility by not addressing the issue. If I had it to do all over again, I would have admitted my error to the jury, asked them to ignore that particular evidence and look to all the other evidence that I had of the company's weak financial condition. If a single broken promise can hurt your credibility, then multiple broken promises are deadly, causing the jury to tune you out altogether as unreliable.

No matter how you try to connect with the jury, always remember that the ultimate goal is to have them identify with your client. In a sense, you are an extension of your client, so you've succeeded in using pathos

---

1. Generally, from Daniel Christensen, "Select the right jury for your case: here's how to root out bias among potential jurors during voir dire to strengthen your client's chance of a fair trial," *Trial*, April, 2004.

even if the connection you've made with the jurors is between them and you, rather than between them and your client. In either case, once the connection is made, you have taken a huge step toward winning the case.

CHAPTER 7

Maintaining Credibility Through Cross-Examination

> "In cross-examination, as in fishing, nothing
> is more ungainly than a fisherman pulled
> into the water by his catch."
> —*Louis Nizer, noted trial lawyer and author*
> *of the forward to the Warren Commission*

Cross-examination is one of the best places to cement your credibility. It's also viewed as one of the most exciting and dynamic moments in a trial. Why? Because it's the advocate versus the witness. If the witness wins, it can destroy your case. If the advocate prevails, you enhance your credibility and continue to move the jury to your side of the fence. In the next few pages, we'll look at methods to build your credibility and defeat the witnesses.

The Three Techniques of Cross-Examination

There are three basic cross-examination techniques or tools: (1) impeaching; (2) hitchhiking; and (3) limiting. All are available to the cross-examiner in implementing his purposes. But just as a hammer is not the appropriate tool for every project, lumping these techniques together or limiting yourself to only one is a mistake. So let's examine all three.

A. Impeaching

The single most common error during cross-examination is assuming that every cross-examination should attempt to impeach the adverse witness. Automatically reaching for impeachment whenever you cross-examine is an error of fundamental importance and lethal consequence because you will fail to impeach a witness a significant percentage of the time. Why is this failure a lethal error? Whenever you attack the credibility of a witness and fail, you impeach your own credibility.

Why do so many lawyers attempt to impeach? Because they see only the huge upside of cross-examination. The more hostile the witness has been on direct examination, and the more harmful he has been to your case, then the more serious the blow to him and your adversary when you impeach him. If you can demonstrate that he lied or did not know what he was talking about, the harm to your adversary goes well beyond the loss of the witness. Whenever a witness is shown to have deliberately lied, that blow harms both the witness and the lawyer who called him. Unless your opponent can disassociate himself from the impeached testimony of his own witness by demonstrating ignorance or some other means, such a blow can even be fatal to your opponent's case. Lawyers seek to impeach because it's the grand slam of trial work. It's exciting, it's flashy, and, if done successfully, it can lead to a huge victory.

What many lawyers fail to realize is that there is also a huge downside. When you pick a credibility fight with a witness during cross-examination, you wager your own credibility as well as the witness's. The ante for the cross-examination battle is the same for both the cross-examiner and the witness: credibility. When you ask "Isn't it true that you were in Denver on June 20, 2008?" and both the witness and the jury answer "No," then the cross-examiner has done everything to himself that he sought to do to his adversary. He has wagered and lost some of his own credibility by making an assertion of truth in the form of a question that the jury has rejected.

Truth #1: Impeachment or cross-examination forces the cross-examiner to wager his credibility against the credibility of the witness and the adverse lawyer. For that reason, impeachment and credibility attacks should be reserved for last, not first.

So many attorneys view cross-examination as "Nothing ventured, nothing gained. I will try something and if it does not work, I will try something else." They seem to believe that credibility attacks on the witness that fail are costless to the attacker. They're wrong.

Truth #2: Impeachment should be employed only in two circumstances:

(a) When you absolutely have to (i.e., if the witness's testimony is believed, you will lose the case)

(b) When you're pretty sure you can bring it off successfully.

So unless you will lose the case without impeachment or are positive you can win the credibility battle, generally look to one of the other techniques of cross-examination.

In civil cases, almost invariably you'll have to attack the credibility of adverse parties. A civil litigant does not willingly admit that judgment should be entered against him in the amount claimed, or that his own claim for damages is overstated. With narrow exception, the adverse party in a civil case will force a credibility confrontation, and therefore a credibility attack, because if the witness's testimony is believed, he'll win the case. Impeachment of such a witness is virtually always required simply because there is no way to avoid it. And while hitchhiking and limiting can also be employed, neither one alone or in combination will likely carry the day if your adverse party leaves the witness stand believed.

Read any work on cross-examination and you'll encounter the admonishment that the cross-examined witness must be kept under control. That is, he should be held to "yes" or "no" answers; he should never be allowed to make lengthy responses or explanations. If he volunteers information that goes beyond the narrow confines of the questions, then you should appeal to the judge to strike the answer or admonish the witness against voluntary answers. I disagree with all of that in principle, and in practice have found it utterly impractical.

Whenever a lawyer tries to force a witness to answer in just one word, the lawyer sends a clear signal to the entire courtroom that he's afraid of the witness and what the witness has to say about his case. In turn, it destroys the lawyer's ability to convince the jury that she is a truth-giver interested in justice rather than a game-player interested only in winning. On the other hand, I certainly do not recommend opening up the record and giving the witness free rein to say what he wants, when he wants.

So how do we walk between these two extremes? First, the cross-examiner controls the topics of the testimony by the selection of the subject matter of the questions. Second, the cross-examiner controls the witness by punishing him if he volunteers or fails to answer.

The simple lack of common courtesy, as well as the gamesmanship, in demanding only "yes" or "no" answers is so apparent to everyone in the courtroom that anyone who has ever tried this "yes" or "no" technique has not been able to do so without feeling guilty. You feel guilty because you know what you are doing is not polite. In fact, it is mean, harsh, and unfair. I've heard lawyers try to ameliorate these feeling by explaining to the witness that the questions have been "carefully crafted" so that the witness need only respond with "yes" and "no" answers. Then they will compound the problem by telling the witness that his lawyer will have an opportunity to ask additional questions and let him explain anything. Why? Because this speech and similar instructions hurt your credibility, emphasizing that you do not want to hear, much less deal with, the whole truth.

Truth #3: The attorney who will not permit a witness to make an explanation, and instead insists on oneword answers and smothers anything he does not want to hear, destroys his own credibility in the process.

If you do not insist on one-word answers, however, some witnesses will abuse the process by volunteering material that's simply not called for by the question, often in a partisan effort to reach out and hurt your case. For example:

Q: You recognized the driver in the car, didn't you?
A: Yes.
Q: It was Frank Jones, wasn't it?
A: Yes. He was weaving and looked drunk.

Now that answer was totally inappropriate and exceeded the bounds of the questions. Most commentators suggest that you should appeal to the judge to instruct the witness to answer only the question asked. I disagree for three reasons. First, it gives your opponent an opportunity to argue his case in responding to the objection. Second, the judge may agree with your opponent and overrule the objection. Third, the examiner shows weakness by asking the judge for help and passing up an opportunity to employ self-help or discredit the witness. When a witness volunteers information, it can only be of two kinds. The information either is relevant and thus legally admissible or is evidence that the examiner has a legal right to keep out of the record. Let's take a look at how to deal with each of these.

If the blurt-out is legally in the case, as in the above example, then the only objection the examiner has is "nonresponsive" because it was not called for by that particular question. No matter what you do, you will be forced to deal with that testimony sooner or later. Even if you are successful in striking the answer from the record, the victory is brief because the jurors have heard it, and I guarantee you they will hear it again on redirect. And if he says it again on re-redirect, you absolutely must deal with it in on re-cross. Therefore, if a witness blurts out nonresponsive harmful information, you must deal with it then and there without running from it or whining to the judge for help. How is it done?

Step One: Make it clear to the jury that the witness cheated. Reap the benefit of the blurt-out by pointing out that the witness was not supposed to answer in such a way. When a witness blurts out, he opens himself up to attack. By deliberately exceeding the bounds of a question during cross-examination, the witness reveals himself to be a partisan and makes it possible for the cross-examiner to wound his credibility. You job is to demonstrate that the witness has cheated, and that the witness did so because he is partisan. How? By immediately repeating the same question in exactly same words. Why? To immediately demonstrate that the witness is cheating. And if the witness does it again, you should repeat the same question in the exact same words again. Indeed, the more the witness repeats the excessive answer, the better it is for you because the repeated fouls will make it clearer to the jury. Watch:

Q: You recognized the driver in the car, didn't you?

A: Yes.

Q: It was Frank Jones, wasn't it?

A: Yes. He was weaving and looked drunk.

Q: It was Frank Jones who was driving the car, wasn't it?

A: Yes, I told you, and he was weaving and looked drunk.

Q: My question to you, sir, is, it was Frank Jones who was driving the car, wasn't it?

If the jurors see what's going on—and sooner or later they will—this exchange has just made it easier for the cross-examiner to immediately thereafter go after the assertion that Frank Jones was drunk. You have just established that the source of that assertion is not a neutral or impartial witness, but someone who has taken the witness stand with a mission and a purpose. You have given the jurors a reason to be suspicious of the witness. Once this is done, the rest becomes easier.

It's essential for you to demonstrate the unfairness of the witness's answer yourself. If you ask the court reporter to read back the question to the witness instead of immediately repeating the question, too much time will elapse. Court reporters rarely find anything quickly. The moment will be lost.

If you appeal to the judge, not only will you lose the opportunity to deal with the foul yourself, but you'll send an invitation to your adversary to get involved in the dialogue with the judge. Then, anything can happen and nothing will happen as immediately as if you do it yourself. Of course, if you repeat the question, your adversary (direct examiner) may insert himself anyway. He may object to what he will call harassing the witness when you repeat the question. And if that happens, the judge's response will be equally unpredictable, but this much is absolutely certain: if the witness keeps on volunteering, and you keep on repeating the questions to demonstrate the unfairness of the witness, sooner or later your adversary will stop interfering.

Step Two: Deal with the merits. After demonstrating the witness's bias, you must immediately deal with the merits—the truth or falsity of the statement. This assumes that you have something at your disposal that deals with the volunteered material. But whether or not you possess something to counter with, you're better off following this path, because you have at least damaged the witness by showing bias. And if that is all that can be done, at least that is something.

When a witness volunteers an answer that is nonresponsive and information that is not properly in the record, containing material that you have a right to have excluded from the case, then you must object and move to strike and/or request a limiting instruction. These requests have nothing to do with erasing the material from the minds of the jurors. It's based on legal technicalities. An unresponsive answer that is not objected to and not stricken is in the record. All objections to it are waived. It becomes legal evidence that may be utilized later in the trial during summation or even on appeal.

Truth #4: When a witness on cross-examination volunteers improper evidence, you must object and move to strike. On the other hand, answers that are admissible but unresponsive should immediately be dealt with by you.

Don't Be Afraid to Deal with Adverse Testimony and Adverse Witnesses. The underlying foundation for all of this faulty, "over-control the witnesses" advice is fear. Fear that the witness may indeed say something on the stand, anticipated or not, that will hurt the cross-examiner's case. The simple fact is that the jury expects that the advocate who is "in the right" will not manicure testimony, run from issues, or flinch before adverse witnesses. A frightened or overcareful advocate is not the standard-bearer of an honest case.

You should seize the opportunity that leading questions offer to argue your case, but the ability to lead is not an excuse to smother, to stifle, or to run from adverse testimony and witnesses. Bad facts and bad witnesses must be dealt with in a direct way, a way that conveys honesty and security in one's own case. Just because a witness makes an assertion does not mean that it will be believed, especially if you have a question that will address or respond to the bad fact. When I used to play peekaboo with my daughter, she would cover her eyes to hide from me. Her logic was the simple logic of a two-year-old: if she could not see me, then I must not be able to see her either. Well, we all know the logical fallacy of that.

Similarly, if the advocate closes his eyes to the bad facts (by not addressing them) or stops the bad facts from coming out (by interrupting the witness describing a bad fact in midsentence and saying "Your lawyer will have a chance to ask you questions"), does the bad fact go away? No. In fact, the advocate's action has the opposite effect: it only focuses the jury's attention on the bad fact and the advocate's unwillingness to address it. In short, avoiding bad facts, rather than taking them on and showing how they do not affect the outcome of the case, will only give greater effect to the hurtful testimony.

Truth #5: Adverse statements by witnesses do not hurt unless they are believed.

The jury sees the confrontation between an adverse witness and you as a kind of contest. Jurors are unimpressed by an advocate who runs from that confrontation. Jurors don't expect to believe, nor will they believe, everything a witness says from the stand. But they do expect the advocate to confront adverse testimony on the issues before them, and they do decide whether to believe the witness as they listen to him. They do not store up information like computers, withholding their credibility judgments for the end of the case. They vote on every question and answer, then and there. By the end of the case, days, weeks, or even months later, the jurors may not remember every witness or much of what any one witness said. The votes of the jurors on the underlying facts, as to what they believe happened, were cast much earlier. The jurors vote as they listened first to the opening and then to the first witnesses. The beliefs they formed early on became a factor in their later judgments and votes as additional testimony was given by the ensuing witnesses as the trial went forward.

For these reasons, the importance of the advocate begins to fade after the early moments of the trial. At the beginning, all that the jurors have to base their initial reaction upon is the advocates—what the lawyers say in opening and how they say it. Soon thereafter, however, the witnesses and the exhibits appear. From that point on, the jurors have more than contesting advocates to go on. And although their own biases will by then have been influenced by the earliest moments of the trial, enormously complex forces come into play. Their views on the subjects were already well formed, and the more evasive the answer, the more those views will harden and the witness's credibility will plummet. On the other hand, the failure to take issue with the witness is more lethal to the examiner than a possible bad answer from the witness.

When the cross-examiner's statement to the jury through the witness, and the witness's answer to the jury through the examiner do not agree, the jury votes on the question and answer immediately. The juror agrees either with the examiner's assertion or the witness's denial. No one waits to vote, as in the following example:

Q: Isn't it a fact that you were in Chicago on May 11?
A: No.

The juror votes then and there. He does not wait for the next witness or the summation at the end of the trial. Jurors do not reserve their judgment until the end of the day. They don't even pause for the conclusion of the examination before casting their ballots. They vote on the assertion in the question and the denial in the answer as they hear it. The votes may change later, but they are cast. Once cast, the longer held, the more difficult it will be to change them. It's therefore essential that you win that ballot on the assertion and the denial then and there. Each contest over each question is like a bet, and the stakes are your credibility versus the witness's. So in Aristotelian terms, the ethos of both the lawyer and the witness are at stake.

Cross-examination, then, is the attorney putting questions in series to the witnesses. These questions, looped together, put forth the advocate's position to the jurors, a position they will accept or will reject . . . and their votes will be cast immediately. Cross-examination is not a combination of episodic jabs taken at the witness, the effectiveness of which the jury will judge by the time the case is summed up. Cross-examination is an exchange by two people (sometimes in dialogue, sometimes in confrontation) that the jurors judge immediately.

Cross-Examination versus Direct Examination. While neither direct nor cross is merely a vehicle to plant material into the record for later use when you sum up, there is a basic difference between them. During direct, the jurors will be synthesizing all of the information to determine what the lawyer is trying to convey to them through this witness. During cross, on the other hand, because you can lead, the jurors should have no difficulty understanding what you're saying to them through the witness. The difficulty lies elsewhere. You now have an uncooperative witness who, unlike your witness on direct, is more likely to disagree with the assertions in your questions. This difficulty leads us to the greatest power of the cross-examiner—the power to select where you will do battle without regard for the chronology of events of the case and the linear organization of direct examination. So the problem on cross-examination is to develop the skills and the technique necessary to prevail while maintaining your credibility during the particular fights that you choose to pick with the witness on the stand.

While the examiner on direct loops key ideas, repeating his witness's answers in his next question to emphasize them, repetition by the lawyer on cross is an unfailing sign of a lawyer in trouble. If you repeat an answer without dealing with the answer or the witness, you lose. For example:

Q: Isn't it true, Ms. Jones, that before you signed the contract, you read it?

A: No.

Q: It's not true that before you signed the contract, you read it?
A: No.
Q: I see. Well, let me ask you [about something else].

In this example, the attorney chose to make an assertion. The witness denied it. What are the jurors to think? Who will they vote for? No one can tell. Why? The attorney did not follow up. She gave the jurors no way to resolve the factual disagreement between counsel and the witness. Moreover, her failure to deal with the witness's denial, coupled with her repetition of that denial, simply emphasizes the testimony, reinforces the witness's victory, and confirms that the examiner has nothing with which to deal with the witness's position. When this happens, the gambit is lost, you fail to make your point, and your credibility is diminished.

The fundamental error of the illustration lies in the cross-examiner's selection of the topic for confrontation.

Truth #6: The cross-examiner should never make an assertion he is not prepared to vindicate, and preferably immediately.

When you have nothing to confront or impeach the witness with, then you have nothing to demonstrate to the jurors that the witness has just answered falsely. You stand helpless and defenseless against the witness. And so, like the prizefighter momentarily stunned by a blow who goes into a clinch, our hypothetical lawyer hides her confusion and buys time to recover by simply repeating the last answer and thereby doubling the blow. The juror is again left to his immediate vote with the lawyer echoing the witness's testimony and nothing more.

As in the case of a witness volunteering information that is harmful to your case, when a witness makes a denial that you can deal with, you must deal with it then and there. Suppose, for example, you have an affidavit in which the witness has admitted that he did read the contract that he has denied reading on direct. Then, you must show this inconsistency to the jurors immediately after eliciting the denial.

Q: Isn't it true, Mr. Jones, that before you signed the contract, you read it?
A: No.
Q: Mr. Jones, isn't it a fact that in your affidavit of June 12, 2004, you swore, and I quote: "I read the contract and then I signed it"?

By doing this, you vindicate your position and demonstrate to the jury that you are reliable and win the credibility wager against the witness.

Of course, you may not have a document or prior testimony or anything physical to impeach the witness with, but you may have a witness who was present and who is prepared to testify that he saw Jones go through the contract. The trouble is that this impeaching testimony may not be heard for days or even weeks after Jones has left the stand, and by then the jury will have long since voted on that question and answer. Certainly, the votes are subject to change. But by the time you finally get around to calling your impeaching witness, the subject must be resuscitated. It must be recalled in the minds of jurors who have long since voted. It's better to deal with the subject while it's still alive than to try to bring it back from the dead.

It requires more skill to immediately confront a witness with other witnesses who have not yet testified than to instantly confront the witness with his own prior inconsistent testimony or an impeaching document. But in order to make the confrontation immediate and to let the jurors know that you are not puffing, bluffing, or fishing, it's essential to do so, and to do so without violating the rules against referring to something not in evidence, or the rule against asking the witness to comment on the veracity of another. Yet it can be done.

Q: Isn't it true, Mr. Jones, that before you signed the contract, you read it?

A: No.

Q: Now, Mr. Brown was with you in that room when you signed the contract, correct?

Now Jones has a problem. He can admit the assertion or he can deny it, but either way the jury can now appreciate that you have some evidence to support your assertion and this will add to your credibility. If Jones answers "No," he might be asked if he knows of any reason why Brown would claim to have been there when Jones says he wasn't. If Jones answers the question about Brown's presence "Yes," he might be asked whether he knows of any reason why Brown would say Jones read the contract if he had not. Good trial lawyers may debate whether these last questions about Brown's motivations are permissible. However, the important point is that the cross-examiner, having selected the topic and the point of conflict, must not willingly abandon the field, leaving the issue undecided, at least not if he has the means to show the jury that he is correct in his position and assertion. And if he has no such means, the cross-examiner should not have picked the fight to begin with.

Truth #7: The greatest power of cross-examination is the ability to pick the subject of confrontation with the witness. These selections should be determined by the cross-examiner's assessment of his ability to make his point, and to prevail in the confrontation he selects. This will be determined by the material the cross-examiner has at hand to cross-examine with.

What I call weapons of discipline are physical and testimonial evidence that can be employed to contradict the witness's direct testimony or to compel him into agreement on cross. They are the greatest tools of the cross-examiner. The best-known method of impeachment is the use of inconsistent material, usually, although not always, in the form of prior inconsistent statements. Most pretrial depositions are conducted for two reasons: (1) to discover what the person will say at trial and (2) in a case of an adverse witness or party, to develop impeaching material for trial. The simple truth is that all witnesses are likely to testify somewhat differently if called to trial to repeat their account after months and years have intervened since the time of their pretrial deposition. No one's memory is good enough to tell the same story without the slightest variation in two or more instances, at least not unless the tale has been literally memorized, word for word. By the same token, no reasonable juror expects immaculate consistency from people they listen to. None of us are suspicious of minor variations in accounts given months apart. Such minor variations do not indicate falsity. In fact, they may be the very trademark of sincerity.

One hallmark of unsuccessful cross-examination is the harping upon meaningless and petty inconsistencies between prior and present testimony of the same witness. This type of cross-examination signals that the examiner has nothing significant to discredit the witness. Juries understand and are even forgiving of such minor inconsistencies, usually explained away with statements that at the deposition "I was nervous" or "I was scared." For that reason, the direct examiner is well-advised not to attempt to repair or even to address such minor inconsistencies on cross. The harm to the cross-examiner who pounces upon such petty nonsense will far exceed any minor damage he may even hope to do with the witness.

Of course, even small inconsistencies can be hurtful to credibility if there are enough of them. Testimony that is riddled with mistakes and errors is at best unreliable, and at worst a fabrication. If you can develop a sufficient number of inconsistencies, mistakes, or failures of the witness to recall details he is expected to remember, then attack him as unreliable. But the point remains that though no major inconsistency should be overlooked, isolated and petty errors of the witness should be left alone. And that brings us to the important issue of how to prepare, organize, and deliver a cross-examination when you do have inconsistent statements of a witness.

No one can hope to confront a witness with his prior inconsistent testimony unless those prior statements are ready at hand. If the witness hits you with an inconsistency and you delay your attack fumbling to find the deposition and the right page and line to vindicate your assertion, all is lost as the jurors' attention wanders off to important issues in their lives like how to get little Billy to soccer or what's for dinner. In order to pull off impeachment, the attorney must be able to crisply and cleanly vindicate his assertion. That means you have to have the deposition ready and all of your impeachment material indexed for speedy retrieval and use. The first rule of such an index is that you, the cross-examiner, must do the indexing. An index will not serve well if done by the hand of another. It's the very labor of indexing that gives the examiner the familiarity with the material necessary to use it instantly and capably.

The moment has finally arrived. The witness upon the stand has testified directly contrary to his prior testimony or in direct conflict with physical exhibits. You have the prior contrary testimony at hand, ready to impeach. What happens next? Most cross-examiners do the wrong thing. They begin an elaborate incantation and windup to set the witness up for what they believe will be the crushing blow, rather than just stepping right up and belting him.

A typical scenario goes something like this. The witness has testified that the light was red. One year before, she swore in deposition that it was green. Now the witness has opened herself to an attack and the attorney smells blood. But he does not go in for the kill. Instead, the examiner starts an elaborate verbal windup. The problem with the windup is that the jury ends up forgetting what the attorney got all excited about in the first place and the jury's attention is lost. Watch:

Q: You say to this jury that the light was red.

A: Yes.

Q: Do you remember a year ago, you came to my office?

A: Yes.

Q: Do you remember that your lawyer was there?

A: Yes.

Q: Do you remember a court reporter there?

A: Yes.

Q: Do you recall that you took an oath there to tell the truth just as you did before this jury?

A: Yes.

By this time, the cross-examiner is warmed up and excited about the series of "yes" answers, but the only people in the courtroom who are concerned are the witness and the adverse lawyer. The jurors have either fallen asleep or gotten lost. This colloquy makes no sense to jurors. They are not eagerly waiting for the blow that the cross-examiner is winding up to deliver. In fact, they have probably forgotten just what piece of testimony the cross-examiner is in the process of attacking.

Conversely, the witness has not forgotten. Her own attorney (if he is worth his salt) has prepared her and told her what this windup will lead to. Therefore, the witness's mind is racing. Assuming that the contradiction has not been handled on direct, the witness is mentally paging through her prior testimony wondering what she said in her deposition and why the cross-examiner is so excited. And if the witness reaches the correct reference before the cross-examiner finally delivers his pitch, the witness will volunteer the explanation before the accusation can be fully made, stealing any thunder the cross-examiner may have had. Watch:

Q: Now I took your deposition in May.

A: Yes

Q: The accident had occurred only six months earlier.

A: Yes.

Q: Now, I am sure you will agree that your memory was better then than it is now, a year later.

A: No, not necessarily for me, I must admit. You see, I was nervous, frightened, and scared during the deposition because I had never testified before.

The cross-examiner has lost the exchange before he even finishes his warm-up, but he presses on. Although the witness did not continue and explain the inconsistency in his deposition before the accusation, the examiner now makes certain that the witness fully appreciates the inconsistency and has every chance to win the game before the examiner.

Q: I am going to hand you your deposition.

A: O.K.

Q: I want you to read it to yourself and not out loud before I ask you another question.

And, now the witness reads. Even if she has failed to remember her entire testimony while the examiner was giving her every opportunity, she now knows what it is. She sees the inconsistency because the examiner has just shown it to her. The witness begins to mentally formulate her excuses, which she will probably even volunteer before the impeachment question is uttered. And if the witness has not finished formulating her defense when the questioner is ready to pounce, she may obtain further delay by claiming not to have finished reading. What are the jurors doing all this time? Do you think that they still have the original premise in mind and are sitting on the edge of their seats waiting for the final blow? Not likely. More likely, they are lost in thoughts far, far away from the courthouse, and the point you are trying to make either never gets made or falls on deaf, inattentive ears.

Truth #8: Just as it is vital for the accused to make the explanation before the accusation is heard or is even known, it is vital for the accuser to make his accusation before it can be explained away.

Thus, the accusation on cross-examination is put entirely in one question, so that the witness has no chance to speak before the accusation is fully made, heard, and appreciated by the jurors. Watch:

Q: Ms. Brown, is it a fact that you just swore to this jury that the light was red against Mr. Jones, at the time of the accident, but that in your deposition, page 12, line 13, you swore [and then visibly hold the deposition up and read from it to further build your credibility for accuracy and truth]:

Q: What color was the light?

A: It was green.

[Only then walk to the witness and place the transcript on the podium before the witness.]

With that one question, you have done it, and done it the way a young Mike Tyson would have done it. Nothing tricky, no fancy footwork, just get close and punish your opponent with short, lethal shots from the shoulder.

Some may object that this approach violates Rule 613(a). For our purposes, this rule is superfluous. The model offered above satisfies Rule 613(a) because the witness is not required to answer before she is shown the prior statement. The prior statement is put into her hands before she answers. The showing is not a private one between the examiner and the witness. The contents are openly displayed, orally, to the jury at the same time they are given to the witness, but before she answers and before she can defeat the accusation by volunteering an answer.

Why did this windup business come to pass? It lies in our natural reluctance to immediately enter direct controversy and instead hedge our bets. In other words, just as we try to warm ourselves up with a slow lead-in to the case in our opening, we tend to warm up before a direct confrontation with the witness on cross-examination. Then we make up excuses for this reluctance and rationalize ourselves into accepting those excuses. We tell ourselves that the jurors need these windups to understand the trial process and to alleviate their fears. We seize on that nonsense to excuse our need to calm our fears with five minutes of canned beginning before getting to the heart of the opening. And now we see the same rationalizing (that it's really the jury and not the lawyer that needs a windup) to justify our reluctance to immediately impeach the witness with his prior inconsistent testimony.

For example, I've heard lawyers maintain that before using a prior inconsistent deposition, it's necessary to first explain what a deposition is, and to show that a court reporter and another lawyer were in attendance at the time or else the jurors won't understand the significance of prior inconsistency. Once again, we kid ourselves that we're postponing the confrontation for the benefit of the jurors. If you anticipate that you will need to impeach a witness, and you think the jury needs a preview explanation, provide that explanation in voir dire. Be sure to explain that a deposition is testimony taken under oath and recorded word-for-word by a court reporter prior to the trial, and that the witness had his lawyer present, and the testimony is just like it was given here in court. If you can't afford to waste precious time in voir dire on such an explanation, ask the court to give the same or similar instruction before any trial testimony is taken.

Let's face it: We do these windups for ourselves, not for the jurors. No matter how long you go on with your preliminary windup, you're not likely to make the deposition process clear to the jurors, even if the jurors really cared about such matters. The intricacies of the deposition process are not likely to hold the jurors' attention. And there is no reason for them to be concerned with such matters. What they do care about is that the witness told two different stories while under oath. And they are more likely to care about that if you can deliver that message directly, while you still have their attention and before the witness has drawn the poison by offering excuses.

The whole purpose of your index of a witness's prior statement is to be able to punish a witness who deviates or to drive him to say what you wish. And that is why I call indexes weapons of discipline. You will use them to discipline a misbehaving and untruthful witness. Therefore, you must have the actual pages of the witness's prior testimony photocopied and physically grouped together, point by point, although obviously you have extracted only the significant material. If the witness contradicts his prior testimony on direct, your material is ready. In this regard, you should take special care with the kind of notes you make during the direct as you wait to cross.

First, your notes for cross-examination should never be questions you will ask. This is true both for the notes you make in your office while looking ahead to the upcoming direct and cross and for the notes you will make as you listen to the direct in court. As you listen to the direct, you should make notes only as to what you intend to confront the witness with on cross-examination. There is no point in writing about what you will not use. Also, your courtroom notes should be as close as possible to the words of the witness that you intend to confront on the cross-examination. Typically, your question on cross-examination, if it is to address what the witness said on direct examination, may begin with, "Now, Mr. Jones, on direct you told this jury _____, but isn't a fact that on page 9, line 12 of your deposition, you swore that _____?"

What if the witness on direct examination has not contradicted himself? Is your index then valueless? Absolutely not. Your index is a tool you can use to force the witness on the stand to answer consistently with his prior testimony at the pain of being impeached. Your index is a tool to develop lines of cross-examination designed to force the witness to agree with the assertion of your so-called question. And your index, coupled with the notes you made on his direct testimony, is the weapon of discipline you use to drive the witness back into line when he strays. In this form, you do not wind up to a prior inconsistency, for there is no windup. You simply state your proposition and then hit the witness with the deposition testimony or the impeaching evidence if he does not agree with your assertion, or if he gets out of line when answering. Watch:

> **Q:** Now, on May 11, you were in Chicago?
>
> **A:** No.
>
> **Q:** Do you recall being asked this question in your deposition at page 2, line 4, "Where were you on May 11," and you answered under oath, "I was in Chicago."

or

> **Q:** I am giving you a "paid" stamped bill in your name from the Hilton Hotel in Chicago, dated May 11, and ask you, "Isn't it a fact that you were in Chicago on May 11?"

Mastery of the use of weapons of discipline in cross-examination is vital, because one of the great errors of cross-examination is the asking of questions without the power to compel agreement or to punish deviation.

I offer you this example from a case I tried several years ago to demonstrate how the proper use of weapons of discipline will enhance your credibility. The case involved a nuisance claim. Thirteen landowners claimed that my client's facility was so loud and so ugly that it constituted a nuisance. Because all 13 were parties, the "Rule" did not apply to them and many of them sat through the trial. By sitting through the trial, they had witnessed me repeatedly impeach prior plaintiffs with their prior deposition testimony. When I went for my deposition to impeach the fifth witness (as modeled above), he cut me off and said, "Mr. Cox, you know the record better than I do, and if you say that is what I said, then that is what I said." It may not seem like a major admission, but if you believe, as I do, that the advocate's credibility is one of the keystones of a successful trial, then you cannot ask for a better testimonial to your credibility than one from the mouth of your opposing party. The entire jury heard the witness admit that I knew the evidence better than he did, solidifying one of the main goals of advocacy: to be perceived as the truth-giver in the courtroom.

Truth #9: If you do not have the material (the physical stuff) to make the witness answer your way at the pain of being impeached, then you should avoid the confrontation.

Most commentators deal with the subject of cross-examination designed to attack a witness's character or integrity as a separate subject, arguing that such interrogations are sufficient in and of themselves to overcome the direct examination of the witness. I must respectfully disagree.

Attacking witnesses' integrity is nothing but an element of the technique of impeachment. After all, cross-examination about prior misconduct is aimed at demonstrating to the jury that the witness is lying as to some or all of the facts of the case. To that end, character attacks may—like attacks on witnesses as to bias—help a cross-examiner deal with evidence offered by the witness as to the facts of the case. But in most instances, such cross-examination does not completely remove the need of the cross-examiner to deal at some point with any damaging testimony that the witness has offered. Any prosecutor will tell you that he has seen innumerable prosecution witnesses whose character had been impeached with great success, and the jury convicted the defendant anyway. Successful cross-examination must do more than show that the witness is the kind of person who could lie, or even one who would lie. Truly outstanding cross-examination illustrates with evidence that the witness has in fact lied about this case while on the stand. The success of a character attack in the first half is simply designed to facilitate success in the second, impeachment half.

In civil cases today, the opportunity to attack the general character and integrity of a witness has been greatly diminished by the Rules. But even if those rules did not exist, an advocate who does nothing but attack the witness, totally ignoring what the witness has to say about the case on trial, is not doing his job. It's not enough to demonstrate that a witness is the kind of person who would lie. You must use that achievement to help you demonstrate that (1) he has told at least some lies in the case itself and, preferably, (2) at least one of these lies is material to the case. Once a witness has been shown as a person who would lie, you must offer the jury some indication that the witness had in fact lied about what happened in this case.

Truth #10: Attacking the character and even the reliability of a witness is not usually sufficient standing alone. The cross-examiner must directly challenge at least some significant point of the witness's testimony against his case.

Cross-Examination to Bias. Cross-examination designed to demonstrate that a witness has a bias (that is, a reason to lie) is but another technique of impeachment. Very much like attacks on the witness's character, which demonstrates only that the witness has the capacity to lie, such examinations do not demonstrate that the witness has fabricated testimony in this case, only that he may have a motive to do so.

> **Q:** It is true, is it not, Ms. Jones, that you are the business partner of the plaintiff here?

Such a question does not prove a falsehood. Nor does it suggest that the witness is a bad or untrustworthy person. It merely warns that the testimony of such a witness must be closely scrutinized and weighed with great care and caution because of what may be only a subliminal urge on the part of the witness to stretch her testimony in favor of one party, whether or not the witness herself knows that she is stretching things.

All of that is well and good. And if that is all that one has, it is certainly better than nothing. But merely demonstrating that the witness has an interest in the proceedings or the parties is not nearly as effective as coupling that revelation with the demonstration that the witness, while on the stand, has said at least something that is incorrect. And the more "somethings," the better. By something incorrect, I mean something that is not accurate and material. To be sure, if one can show that the witness lied, so much the better. Bias plus mendacity should spell doom. But it can be quite sufficient to show bias plus inaccuracies. This alone may fail to establish that the witness is a deliberate liar, but it may be enough to limit the testimony against your case by persuading the jury to discount that testimony as unreliable.

Although cross-examination can be one of the most difficult tasks in a trial, you should almost never pass up the chance to cross-examine. First, jurors assume that every witness called against you did hurt you, even if, at the moment, they do not quite see how. Second, in the majority of instances, jurors interpret your failure to cross as an inability to do so, not that there was no need to do so. Occasionally, it is true, the direct has been so wide of the mark that "No questions" accompanied by a shrug or a smile may do. But the advocate must never assume that the jurors have recognized that the direct has no value and that there is, therefore, no need to respond. Indeed, the assumption should be just the opposite.

Truth #11: Jurors expect you to deal with every witness called in the case. Your failure to question will not show strength; it is more likely to be interpreted as weakness.

What, then, should one do if a witness has been called to testify and has given no unfavorable testimony? Demonstrate that to the jury with one of the other two techniques of cross-examination.

B. Hitchhiking

Many if not all of the witnesses in any case have at least some information that helps both sides. The truth of this is evident in how we agonize over whether to put the witness on the stand at all: we weigh the help we will get on direct examination against damage we may suffer on cross-examination. Thus, the second technique of cross-examination is to question a witness not to impeach credibility, but instead to extract the favorable facts the witness knows. This technique is sometimes called "hitchhiking," because the examiner climbs aboard the adversary's witness and rides as far as he can in his own direction.

This technique is especially important because in the minds of the jurors, there are never two cases being presented, one for the plaintiffs and one for the defendants. For the jurors, there is only one case. Attorneys for all of the parties are held responsible for everything in the case, no matter when it arises. All are expected to advocate their case through their examinations, regardless of which lawyer called the witness to the stand. This is true whether the attorney happens to be conducting direct or cross-examination, because every witness called to the stand has a great potential for providing at least some helpful information to the cross-examiner's case. The technique of hitchhiking must be considered in planning any cross-examination.

C. Limiting

The third technique of cross-examination is used to render a witness's testimony irrelevant. In other words, this type of examination is designed to make the witness testimony compatible with your theory of the case. This technique is actually used more frequently and successfully than impeachment.

Let's see how to use the limiting technique when impeachment is not an option. Your goal is to use your questions to show the jury that the witness has not hurt you. Watch how it plays out in the exchange below:

> Q: I am correct, am I not, that you have no personal knowledge—
> meaning events you personally saw or heard about the transaction?
> A: Yes.
> Q: For example, you did not personally hear or see the negotiations
> between Mr. Jones and Mr. Smith, did you?
> A: No, I did not.
> Q: So if the main issue that the judge will ask the jury to resolve is
> what took place at the negotiation, you cannot offer any personal
> knowledge to assist their deliberations about what went on dur-
> ing the negotiations?

That last question is one that you need to hold off on until you've earned a certain degree of credibility with the jury. But if you have built up some credibility, the answer to that question doesn't matter, because the jury will agree with your assertion regardless of what the witness says. Your first two questions have demonstrated that this witness has no personal information regarding the central issue of the case. And anything other than complete agreement with your statement will only further harm the witness's credibility. Once you've secured the answer to the first two questions, the third is simply used to connect the dots and make sure the jury understands the limits of this witness's testimony. The witness cannot and did not hurt you, so do not shrink from dem- onstrating that to the jury. Indeed, there is everything to be gained from demonstrating that your adversary has just, at minimum, wasted everyone's time, or at a maximum, tried to pull the wool over everyone's eyes by calling a witness who has nothing to say.

Of course, mere technical witnesses called by your adversary out of legal necessity (perhaps to authenticate a document or to testify to a measurement) may well merit no attention if you are satisfied that the jurors understand the limited and uncontested nature of the testimony. But, saving that, you should assume that the jury expects you to cross-examine and that they will not take silence in your favor.

At the end of the day, whatever method you decide to use whenever questioning a witness should be used with caution and every possible outcome should be "war-gamed" in order to prepare your response. Remember, the jury's opinion of you, as an examiner, is what matters. Today's juror is exposed to television shows such as *Law and Order* and movies that depict larger-than-life trial lawyers who know just what to say to elicit a response that will implicate the guilty party, or clear the wrongfully accused.

CHAPTER 8

The Signaling Principle: What's Next and Are We There Yet?

"A signal is comprehended if it serves to make us notice the object or situation it bespeaks. A symbol is understood when we conceive the idea it presents."
—*Susanne Langer,[1] American philosopher*

As a trial attorney, your opening statement establishes for the jurors the key points you will prove with the evidence and through the witnesses. It sets the tone for what you hope to accomplish. This is your road map, a direction for the trial that will (if everything goes as planned) lead to a successful conclusion, a decision in your favor.

This is where the Signaling Principle first comes into play. Along with your road map, you will use GPS—Giving Pertinent Signals—to let the jurors know your ultimate destination. Jurors want to know why they are here, where you are going, and how you are going to get them there, just as they do when they set the GPS device in their vehicle. You will let them know what comes first, what comes next, and so on, to the end of the trial. This is essentially your outline, an oral outline of the basic organizational flow of your case. Previews allow the audience to pay attention to the content because they already know the structure. Remember, though, that the basic structure of a presentation is not linear, it is circular. Organizational patterns preview the conclusion, as we will see later in this chapter, bringing us back to the beginning.

Here is an example of a speech that gives the audience an outline and signals to watch out for:

---

1. Susanne Langer was an American philosopher who explored the human mind's continuous process of meaning-making through the power of "seeing" one thing in terms of another. Her first major work, *Philosophy in a New Key*, put forth the idea that there is a basic and pervasive human need to symbolize, to invent meanings, and to invest meanings in one's world.

To see how we can end our dependence on fossil fuels, we will first take a look at why we as a society are so dependent upon fossil fuels in the first place; second, we will find out what continues to cause this dependence; third, we will see how ethanol as a fuel supplement will help end this dependence; and, fourth, we will discover how simple it will be to implement this solution and make the world a better place for all of us.

This is one sentence, but it previews the conclusion and each of the supporting points. Let's examine how we can do the same thing in our opening statements.

1. The Opening Statement: Transitions and Signposts

Effective introductions set up the rest of the presentation and create an expectation in the audience of things to come. To meet that expectation, and to keep the presentation working as a coherent whole, all the elements must flow together. To establish flow, transitions allow you to show the connections between all the elements of the presentation, relate all the different parts of the speech to the main purpose, and help the audience see how everything fits together into a complete and coherent package.

At the very least, you will want and need transitions (or signposts, which we will discuss below) between the introduction and the first main point of your presentation, between each of the main points, and then after the last main point and your closing argument.

A signpost is a specific and generally shortened form of a transition. Signposts are quick cues to the audience that the trial presentation is moving from one point to another. Signposts are often short statements such as "first," "second," and "next." They are called signposts because they quickly point out to the jury where we are in the speech. For example:

First, I will establish the connection between Mr. Jones and Mr. Smith, and then I will provide evidence that proves that Mr. Jones had prior knowledge of the terms of the deal before he became involved. By the end of this trial, you will determine (as the evidence proves without a doubt) that Mr. Smith's claims are without merit. I will also establish for you Mr. Smith's true motives for bringing forward this case.

Keep in mind that transitions are more detailed than signposts. Transitions can and do fulfill the same functions as signposts, but they do more and with more detail. Transitions show the connections between all the separate elements of the entire speech. Transitions show the audience the connection between the introduction and the rest of the speech, the connection between each main point, and the connection between the body and the conclusion.

Transitions effectively operate by using two techniques: internal summaries and mini-previews. Later in this chapter we will discuss summary as one of the key functions of a conclusion. Internal summaries take place as transitions between the main points of a speech. An internal summary quickly wraps up the preceding main point before transitioning to the next main point. A mini-preview is simply a shorter version of the main preview from the introduction. A mini-preview follows the internal summary and sets up the next main point.

Transitions are not just verbal. Effective speakers use movement as a transition device. Speakers plan purposeful movement to show the audience, literally, that the speech is "moving" to a new point. In most instances, speakers will start in the center of the room for the introduction, move slightly to one side for the first point, move slightly to the other side for the next point (and so on as needed), and then move back to center for the conclusion. This movement, tied to verbal transition devices, makes it much simpler for the audience to follow the structure of the speech. This means that, from the jury's viewpoint, with each transition you will move to another area of the courtroom. This can also be done through eye contact—the one-thought-per-one-juror concept discussed in Chapter 6.

2. Logos: Developing Your Presentation

> A man asks a cabdriver, "How do I get to Carnegie Hall?"
> "Practice, practice, practice," replies the cabdriver.

Practice is the key to a strong and confident presentation. I advise against memorizing your speech, as it can make you seem stiff or canned. Moreover, it leaves you little flexibility to respond to your opponent's arguments. I focus on becoming familiar with the subjects and topics that

I want to cover and the transition—how I will move from one subject to the next. This way, your practice will prepare you if your opponent does nothing new, but it will also prepare you for maximum flexibility to respond your adversary. Early on in my career when I was dissatisfied with the amount of courtroom presentation time I was getting, I called all the local bar associations across Texas and offered myself as a CLE speaker, looking for at least two every quarter that would allow me to be a presenter. I used those opportunities to practice my personal presentation skills. It wasn't the courtroom, but it was an opportunity to push myself to improve at presenting. In each presentation, I would push myself to try something new, from speaking with no notes to getting out from behind the podium and presenting from different locations in front of and among the audience. Talk about working without a net! It was scary at first, but I lived to tell about it and in the process built my confidence and presentation skills. I encourage you to do the same. Look for opportunities to speak in front of others and use each opportunity to push yourself to the next level as a presenter.

Trial presentation techniques have to be learned through experience. You may want to practice with a written outline until you're comfortable with your presentation.

Once you're satisfied with your familiarity with the presentation, try it without notes. In the trial advocacy classes that I teach at Southern Methodist University School of Law, about halfway through the semester, I will find a student who looks more like he is playing golf, with his head down, than being a trial lawyer, with his head up and connecting. I shake things up by taking his notes away. This is usually followed by stutters and stammers at first, but every single time the student has composed himself by the end of the examination. No one has ever died, but a lot of students have gained new confidence. These are usually the note-deprived students as well as several members of the class who volunteer to try it themselves because they saw a peer complete the exercise successfully.

When I prepare for an argument, I usually outline my presentation in considerable detail for my first practice run. But with each practice round, I rewrite the notes by deleting details and condensing my thoughts. Usually, after several rounds of practice, I can reduce a 30-minute presentation to 10 or 15 key words on a single sheet of paper. I do this for three reasons. First, the practice ensures that I know the material cold. Second, by reducing the detail on the page, it prevents me from reading. Finally, if for some reason I draw a complete blank, I can look down at my notes and find the word that locates me in my presentation and refocuses me on my next thoughts.

The next phase of your preparation should be to deliver your presentation in front of others. When you present it to a room full of strangers, you choose your words more carefully. You do this because you know that they're going to judge you, and your ego won't let you get away with making a fool of yourself. This is where logos comes in. In previous chapters, we discussed how ethos and pathos dealt with people—the former is about the *speaker's* credibility while the latter is about the *audience's* values. But logos is about the message itself. In other words, does your argument hold water?

The best way to test this is to present it to others. And when you do, you have to be willing to take criticism. What's the explanation when someone doesn't understand your argument? Is it their fault for not being smart enough or your fault for not being clear enough? The answer is that it's a trick question—you're always responsible for knowing who your audience is. If you can persuade a room full of rocket scientists, then you should be able to persuade a room full of people without a high school diploma. Your delivery might change, but the underlying message shouldn't. So if your practice audience tells you that some aspect of your argument was unclear, you should be willing to change it.

So what type of practice audience should you use? For trial, your best bet is a lay audience. The most expedient solution might be to gather together a bunch of attorneys from your office to hear your presentation. While this approach gives you the benefit of your partners' cumulative years of experience, it also has some drawbacks. They know too much. The fact that they have a working knowledge of your topic will cloud their ability to judge your presentation as a jury will. They will listen for legal technicalities, for objectionable questions, and for the merits of your case. But a mock jury full of laypersons will actually have to listen to your presentation to determine whether it makes sense. Both types of audiences are valuable, but the lay audience is invaluable.

When you hold a mock trial like this, make it as real as possible. If you have access to a courtroom, use it. Many firms have an actual mock courtroom that they use to let lawyers and witnesses alike get comfortable with the environment. If your firm has the same, great. If not, realize that you can always rent one if your case calls for it. When you're in the courtroom, have the jury sit where they normally would. Make sure your slides and overheads can be read from the back of the room. When you start your mock trial, go into character and stay there. For example, don't stop in the middle of your presentation and ask the mock jury if what you just said made sense or if they have any suggestions. You can discuss all that at the end. Once you're done with the mock trial, set up another one. Even after you're satisfied with the substance and structure of your presentation, keep practicing.

The point of all this practice is that you can't predict how a jury will react to your case, but you can make an educated guess. I recommend never straying from this simple and straightforward advice: "Everything you say and do in your trial presentation must serve the needs of your jury."[2]

When stories are complicated, continuity disappears and the jury again becomes overwhelmed; you cannot connect. Without a clear bond with the audience, your message (and your case) dies on the vine as Juror Overload sets in. Your goal, of course, is just the opposite: to get your jury figuratively or literally to ask "Where or how do I vote?" Ensuring that the jurors track your arguments and want to vote for your arguments is the essence of persuasion. Persuasion is the art of moving your audience from point A (a place of ignorance, indifference, or even hostility) to point B (a place of understanding, action, and advocacy on your behalf). This is done by navigating them through the evidence to the conclusion you seek.

There are three key questions that I focus on answering as I evaluate each argument and piece of evidence I plan to present to the jury. These help me to sort evidence and arguments based on juror benefit. As I consider a theme, a document, a story, or a detail, I ask myself the following three questions:

1. Why am I telling the jury this?
2. How will the jury see this?
3. How can I make this clearer and more memorable to the jury?

---

2. Daniel Christensen, "Select the right jury for your case: here's how to root out bias among potential jurors during voir dire to strengthen your client's chance of a fair trial," *Trial*, April, 2004.

Get to know these questions. If you have questions about whether to present an argument or a piece of evidence, analyze the decision through the lens of these three questions. Use them the next time you prepare for trial as reminders to link every element of your trial presentation to why it matters to jurors and how to make your point clear.

Think about the necessary time lag between the words you speak and the way the jurors are understanding those words. You may think you have the jury's undivided attention—but this is not always true. Even if they spend five seconds making the connection between the document you are discussing and the theme of your case, they are falling behind. And even as they catch up, they will still be behind, because you will have already made your next point. And that's the risk: unless you make your points clearly and assure that your jurors are with you, you will have lost their attention—to the point that the jury stops working so hard to follow the points you're making.

What causes a juror to get lost or confused during a trial presentation? When a reader browses through a book or magazine and encounters a word, reference, or character that is unfamiliar or unclear, the reader simply places a finger on the page and reorients herself by scanning back through the prior pages to find the original definition or reference. The reader has the control and can navigate through the writer's ideas independently. The members of a jury do not have the same control. They are a completely passive audience. They cannot pause the presentation or even ask a question if they're confused or lost. The jury has linear, real-time access to your ideas. That means they can process only one idea at a time. If you go too fast or they struggle with a concept, jurors become lost and disoriented. They are out of the flow and lose focus. They cannot simply put their finger on the current page, retrace their steps, and find their place again. Instead, everything comes to a screeching halt. I liken the jurors' experience to driving through a tunnel and losing the signal on your radio. Somewhere, the DJ is still talking or the music is still playing, but in your car you hear only fuzzy nothingness of static. And just like a lost radio transmission, the juror cannot rewind and catch up. The message is simply lost.

As mentioned previously, there is a direct relationship between your confidence level and your courtroom credibility. To increase your comfort level and confidence, it's a good idea to get to the courtroom about a half hour early and check the following items:

> Sit in the jury box to see what your jury will see.
> Check the room, trial table, and podium. Plan how you're going to set up your workspace.
> Verify that all needed audiovisual equipment is in place and functional, including microphones and videos.
> If you plan to create demonstratives on the fly, make sure you have fresh markers in all the colors you'll need. Then do a test chart and go sit in the jury box again to make sure your words can be seen by the jury.

Until now, we've only discussed your presentation in a general way. The next section will show you specifically how to organize your presentation in a way that makes sense to the jury and may actually keep them excited throughout the trial.

3. Organizing Your Presentation

Organization is much more than the order of information you dispense. It's about realizing that every trial has a narrative. You have to structure your narrative in a way that appeals to the jury and makes logical sense. One way to think about this is to picture your case as a movie. Although the facts may not be sexy, suspenseful, or accompanied by a great soundtrack, question whether you can tell the story in such a way that people would buy tickets to see it.

Some people suggest that you devise a theme and build your case around it. I can't stress how important I think a theme is to your case. But I don't think it should be the starting point in your organizational strategy. First of all, your theme will probably not be self-evident. You may still be thinking about it well into discovery, and you may decide to change it when more facts come to light. Additionally, if you start with your theme and move forward, you run the risk of leaving it behind. Your theme should be a part of your entire case, not just the starting point.

So where do you begin? At the end, of course—the jury charge. Just as everything in a good story is there to lead to the climax, everything in a trial must be there to lead to the jury charge. The vast majority of states use pattern jury charges for every cause of action. Whether you have the burden of proof or not, these pattern jury instructions will tell you what facts you need to prove to establish a claim or defense. So look at your complaint and find the pattern jury charge for your claim(s) or defense(s). Then write down all of the facts of your case that support each issue. On the same list, write down all of the expert opinions you think you'll need as well.

The next step is organizing those facts and opinions into a narrative. In keeping with the analogy, if your entire case is a story, then your witnesses are narrators. Create a chart that lists each fact and opinion, the witness or witnesses who will prove them, and the order in which you want the jury to hear them. The structure of your story can change depending on the witnesses. There are as many ways to put on your case as there are ways to tell a story.

As an example, consider a simple prosecution of armed robbery. Assume for this example that the defendant robbed a convenience store, got into a car with a getaway driver, and the driver was later arrested for some other crime. Assume also that the driver offers to tell the police about the robbery and to testify against the robber in exchange for a lighter sentence. If you, as the prosecutor, wanted to proceed chronologically, you would put the driver on the stand first. He would tell the jury about the plan and the events leading up to the robbery. With this witness, you establish the *mens rea* requirement. Then you could put on the clerk. He would tell the jury about the robbery itself. With this witness, you establish the *actus reus*, the lack of consent, and the value of the thing stolen. Finally, you can put on the investigating officer, who can tell the jury what happened after the robber left the store. The officer can corroborate much of what has already been said, but can also establish other factual requirements (e.g., that the court has jurisdiction by testifying as to the address of the store, that the defendant was read his *Miranda* warnings if that is a defense, and so on).

An alternative way to tell the same story is from the point of view of the officer. This would be more of a detective story, where the jury follows along with the investigation rather than the crime. You present the facts as the officer discovered them, and if the investigation was thorough, the jury should arrive at the same conclusion as the officer—that the defendant is guilty. Here, the officer establishes many of the same factual details as above, and your other witnesses simply corroborate the officer's story. This type of narrative is often preferable because many prosecutors want to start with the most credible witness. Starting with the accomplice (in this instance, the driver) might be dangerous because he can be impeached with the plea deal. With more complex cases, a chronological order may not make sense. For example, imagine that you created a list of 20 facts arranged in the order that they occurred. Assume that one of your witnesses, Albert, can testify to facts 1 through 7 and 16 through 20. Another witness, Betty, can testify to facts 8 through 15. Here, procedural rules may bar you from putting on Albert, then Betty, then Albert again. Thus the solution is to tell two stories—one from Albert's perspective and one from Betty's. Once Albert is finished testifying, the jury should recognize that there is a gap and anticipate you filling it.

A good example of this approach occurs in the film *The Social Network*. The film tells the story of Mark Zuckerberg, the founder of Facebook. Rather than the traditional chronology, this story is framed by deposition testimony in two lawsuits that take place years after the underlying events. As each witness is deposed, he fills in part of the time line and the movie flashes back to the events that the witness is describing. The frame itself is somewhat disjointed. That is, if you cut out all of the flashbacks, what you're left with is a story that jumps back and forth from one deposition to another. But if you cut out the frame and look just at the flashbacks, the story is told chronologically, and the plot is easy to follow.

Here is a good place to make a critical distinction. Although I describe the witnesses as your narrators, this is simply an analogy. You have to be careful not to let your witnesses actually *narrate*. They tell the story, but only through your questions. You have the task of controlling what they say, and more importantly, what they *don't* say. Remember that your witnesses have minds of their own. If you give them free rein to say whatever they please, at best you'll draw an objection (aptly named "narrative"), and at worst they might just say something that loses your entire case.

A great example of this comes from the same movie, where Zuckerberg launches into the following tirade after opposing counsel asks him an open-ended question, allowing Zuckerberg to go on the attack and make his case:

> I think if your clients want to sit on my shoulders and call themselves tall, they have the right to give it a try—but there's no requirement that

> I enjoy sitting here listening to people lie. You have part of my attention—you have the minimum amount. The rest of my attention is back at the offices of Facebook, where my colleagues and I are doing things that no one in this room, including and especially your clients, are intellectually or creatively capable of doing. Did I adequately answer your condescending question?

Although it might make for good drama on the silver screen, every lawyer who has ever defended a deposition probably cringed at the thought of their own client flying off the handle like that.

Once you have plotted your story line, you can start considering your theme. This may be the single most difficult task you face because themes are so hard to find and so easy to screw up. We discussed coming up with a good theme in Chapter 4. But remember that your theme must do three things. First, it must sum up the case in a succinct, memorable way. When the jurors are deliberating, you want them to remember your theme. In fact, you want them to be thinking about the case in terms of your theme. Second, a theme must present the moral of the story. It speaks to the shared values of the community and perhaps those of society at large. Third, it must apply to your case. If you use a theme just because it sounds good, but it doesn't quite fit your facts, your opponent will hammer you with it.

So in coming up with a good theme, your mantra should be: "memorable, moral, applicable." Some cases may require multiple themes. If yours is such a case, you should fully develop each one and keep them distinct. One way to do this is to focus on different themes with each new witness. Another way is to divide your presentation by main ideas and stick to one theme per main idea.

The power of a theme is that it encapsulates your theory of the case within a few words. As a society, our collective attention span has gotten shorter over the last several decades. In the past, lawyers would give two- or three-hour-long closing arguments. Today, the average summation lasts 30 minutes. Clarence Darrow's closing in the infamous Leopold and Loeb case was over 20,000 words. In a world of sound bites, text messages, and Twitter, anything longer than 200 words begins to get boring. This is why the modern trial is no longer a battle of words, but an audiovisual experience. See Chapter 10 for more about putting on a multimedia presentation.

Now that you have your substance (i.e., the facts and theme of the case), you need to start thinking about your structure. How will you tell the story without either boring or confusing the jury? As discussed in Chapter 4, juries retain information better when it's presented both visually and orally. As you prepare your presentation, you must always consider what the jury will see and hear.

There are two main issues to think about when you're dealing with structure—how each part fits within the whole, and how each part connects to another. The first issue is about advancing your theme with each question. You should choose your words carefully to accomplish this goal. For example, if your theme in a medical malpractice case is that the doctor was "too busy to care," then your questions should repeatedly remind the jury how busy the doctor was. Ask your client on direct how long the doctor made her wait and how quickly the doctor rushed through the checkup. Ask the nurses how many patients the doctor had and how many procedures he did in a week. Even if these questions don't go to the heart of malpractice, they instill a thought in the jury—"With all the stuff this doctor had going on, how could he possibly care about any one patient?"

The second issue is about the transitions and internal logic of your presentation. Earlier in this section, we discussed the order of your story. But your story will not be purely narration. In fact, there are four rhetorical modes that we use when telling stories—narration, argumentation, exposition, and description.

As discussed above, narration is the mode that itemizes all the events in a series, whether they have any connection to each other or not. This is a job for your fact witnesses. You know that you're in narration mode when you're asking questions similar to: "And then what happened?"

Your expert witnesses should narrate only to the extent that it is important for the jury to hear what they did to arrive at their opinions. We can easily imagine a psychiatrist, for example, telling the jury that he interviewed the defendant, conducted a Rorschach test, ordered a CAT scan, and so on. But such testimony is only relevant as background information for the expert's opinions. Rather, the important part of the expert's testimony will be exposition. Exposition is the rhetorical mode that deals with analysis. It doesn't answer the question "What happened?," but rather "How did it happen?" Thus, exposition almost always follows on the heels of narration. Say, for example, that you're suing an auto manufacturer for designing faulty brakes. Who would you question first—your client, who can attest to what happened that led to her injury, or the expert, who can attest to the design flaw in the brakes? There are obviously many reasons to put on your client first, but one of those—the one that is relevant to this discussion—is that exposition requires context.

Argumentation, the next rhetorical mode, is your domain, not that of your witnesses. It is the rhetorical mode that is intended to persuade the audience. Rather than portraying an event or analyzing a fact, argumentation tries to instill a point of view in the audience or incite them to act. At trial, the point of view you need to instill is your client's point of view, and the act you want to incite is a favorable verdict. Obviously, the clearest example of argumentation is the closing argument. Another example is the objection—when you or your opponent object, the flow of the narration is interrupted and a small argumentative exchange takes its place.

The last rhetorical mode is description, which doesn't always stand on its own but rather is usually intertwined with one of the other three. For example, after a fact witness testifies that the blue car collided with the red truck in the middle of the intersection, your next question would be "What color was the light?" or "What time was it?" These questions ask the witness to describe the scene surrounding the events being narrated. Similarly, if an expert testifies about the skid marks that the blue car left on the asphalt, he might have to describe their length, thickness, composition, and so on. Such descriptions do not delve into any events, nor do they provide details of *how* something occurred. They simply relate facts, and sometimes facts pertaining to the facts.

It is important to understand the differences between the rhetorical modes because that understanding will help you organize your presentation. When you're in narration mode, for example, it makes the most sense to move chronologically through the events of the case. When you're in exposition mode, however, it will often make more sense to proceed via a cause-effect analysis. For example, if you ask an expert what normally happens when someone presses down on the brake pedal, his response might be that the pressure causes brake fluid to flow into the brake cylinder. That answer may not necessarily describe the next event in the narration, but it does describe the cause-effect relationship at play.

There are other ways to organize your presentation besides chronological and causal. This list describes the more useful organizational schemes:

> **Factual**: describing some circumstance or set of circumstances that support or rebut a fact.
> **Problem-solution**: describing a problem, and providing a solution to it.
> **Procedural**: describing the required steps to accomplish a task.
> **Spatial**: describing the location of things relative to each other.
> **Systemic**: describing how various parts interact with, connect to, or affect each other.

Depending on what you or your witness is going to discuss, any one of these organizational schemes may be better than the chronological scheme.

For each fact on your list, you are going to have to provide supporting evidence. Often a fact will require two or more pieces of supporting evidence, each of which may take on a different organizational scheme. For example, you might use your client's testimony to establish the fact that another driver ran a stop sign and collided with her. Then you would support her testimony with corroboration from eyewitnesses and/or experts. An eyewitness's testimony would likely use the narrative mode, and a chronological organization. That is, the witness would tell a story from his own point of view as to what events took place. But you would also want to ask him some descriptive questions—What time did the accident occur? Which way were the cars going? What was the weather like? These questions can have a spatial or factual organization scheme.

An expert could also be used to corroborate a fact on your list, but the organization would likely be causal or systemic. For example, the expert might testify that the other driver was driving over the speed limit based on her analysis of the skid marks and the collision report. As stated above, the expert's testimony about the techniques she used to arrive at her conclusion could be descriptive or narrative. But her opinions would be expository, because she would be answering the *how* questions rather than the *who*, *what*, *where*, and *when* questions.

Your organizational scheme thus takes on two layers. The first layer is the overarching story line. Each fact is given in a chronological order and originally established by one or more witnesses. The second layer is made up of the supporting evidence, each piece of which supports one or more of the primary facts. This evidence can come from the same witness or witnesses that gave you your story line facts, other eyewitnesses, or experts. Their testimony can take on any organizational scheme that fits what they're testifying to.

Sometimes, all of this will seem disjointed to the jury. It would be nice if you could question all of your witnesses at once, as though they were on a panel. That way, you would have complete control over your story, able to switch fluidly from narration to exposition to description as needed. But because your witnesses can only testify one at a time, you have to place each fact and its supporting evidence in context. So when you ask the expert about her conclusions regarding the other driver's speed, you should make it easier for the jury to remember where her testimony fits within your story. One way to do this is by framing your questions with evidence that has already been admitted. Consider, for example, these alternative questions for an expert witness:

> Based on your analysis, did the defendant run the stop sign?
> Earlier Mr. Smith testified that the defendant ran the stop sign. Did your analysis confirm that testimony?

The second question recalls the earlier testimony from the jurors' memories and helps them to place this testimony within the earlier witness's story.

Another way to achieve the same effect is through demonstratives. Often you need visual or textual help to remind the jurors where you are in your story. Demonstratives are powerful tools that help you maintain your story line even in the most complex cases. In the same example above, you might introduce a map of the intersection during Mr. Smith, and use an enlargement of the same map to help the jury understand the expert's analysis. As discussed above, juries retain information better with a combined audiovisual presentation. But beyond that, the simple fact that you are using the same map that Mr. Smith described will remind the jury how this expert testimony fits within the overall narrative.

Once you have organized your entire presentation, you can work on your opening statement. Earlier in this section, I said that the best place to begin was at the end—to use the jury charge as the framework for your story's outline. Now it's time to end at the beginning. The opening statement should be the last thing you prepare. There are two main reasons for this. First, you can't introduce your story without knowing what it is. If you write an opening statement and then base your presentation on it, you run the risk of forgetting some key fact. You also don't want to be continually revising your opening statement as you add new facts to your story line.

The second reason is that you only want to promise the jury what you can deliver. If you prepare your story line first, you will have a better handle on what evidence may not get in. If there is a good chance that you won't be able to admit something, you don't want to include it in your opening. If you do, and the judge rules against you on its admissibility, your opponent will have a field day with this deficiency during his closing argument.

If everything works as you planned, you will have told a brilliant story. Your opening will present your theme, your theory of the case, and the evidence that you will produce to prove up that theory. Then your witnesses will tell your story for you. Whether it is a chronological story from beginning to end or a patchwork story from multiple points of view, the jury will hear all the facts in a logical order. Your supporting evidence will also make sense in light of the overarching story. The evidence will prove to the jury that your facts are true, and will be placed and organized in a way that does not confuse them. During closing argument, you get to persuade the jury not only that your facts are true in light of all the evidence you presented, but also that their verdict can only go one way because the law dictates it. And at the very end, if you were successful throughout, you will be able to point out to the jury how each and every element of your cause of action, as outlined in their instructions, was met by the facts that you presented.

CHAPTER 9

The Segmentation Principle: People Learn Better When Information Is Presented in Bite-Sized Segments

> "Example is the school of mankind, and they
> will learn at no other."
> —*Kurt Herbert Adler, opera director*

The Segmentation Principle is the basic principle of breaking your information into manageable chunks so that your key points will become sticky. Stickiness is essential to boost your jurors' memory. But you don't want to throw too much information at your jurors at one time. You'll lose them! Hitting the floor at your first opportunity to speak and spraying information around the courtroom at your jury as if firing from an AK-47 will only leave your jurors shocked and overwhelmed. It's an amateur mistake, though one we've all probably made.

Being from Dallas, I like to use Mary Kay Ash as an example for the Segmentation Principle. If you don't know, Mary Kay, in her time, was one of the most influential women in the world. She was the founder of and spirit behind Mary Kay Cosmetics, a worldwide organization that has allowed millions of women to start their own businesses. As the late Mary Kay used to say, "Anyone can eat an elephant one bite at a time." Think of your case as an elephant. Do you expect the jury to swallow it whole in one bite? Break it into small, manageable chunks and spoon-feed your jury at a pace at which they will have no choice but to "get it."

1. The Rule of Three

Whether you're aware of it or not, your life has been governed by a "series of three." When you were a child, this psychological principle was hardwired into your mind. All your favorite stories had a beginning, middle, and end. The number *three* can be found throughout literature, from the canonical works to kids' stories. There were Three Musketeers, Three Little Pigs, Three Billy Goats Gruff, three wishes. Goldilocks encountered three bears, and we all watched the Three Stooges. The races at field day started "Ready, set, go." Even in Sunday school, I was taught about the Father, the Son, and the Holy Ghost. It continues today in our adult lives. Our driving patterns are controlled by the red-yellow-green of stoplights. Athletic teams keep track of wins, losses, and ties.

Why is the Rule of Threes so pervasive? Because it reinforces the idea that a person can only focus his or her attention on three thoughts, goals, or concepts at a time. We remember a list better when it contains a group of three. For example:

> "[W]e cannot dedicate, we cannot consecrate, we cannot hallow, this ground."—Abraham Lincoln, The Gettysburg Address
> "Life, Liberty, and the pursuit of Happiness"—Thomas Jefferson, The Declaration of Independence
> "Duty, Honor, Country"—Gen. Douglas MacArthur, West Point Address of 1962
> "The truth, the whole truth, and nothing but the truth"—part of sworn affirmation made by witnesses before testifying
> Liberté, Égalité, Fraternité (tr. Liberty, Equality, Fraternity)—French national motto
> Citius, Altius, Fortius (tr. Faster, Higher, Stronger)—Olympic motto
> "Veni, vidi, vici" (tr. "I came, I saw, I conquered")—attributed to Julius Caesar

Why is a group of three things so easy to remember? One author explains it this way:[1]

It all comes down to the way we humans process information. We have become proficient at pattern recognition by necessity, and three is the smallest number of elements required to create a pattern. This combination of pattern and brevity results in memorable content.

---

1. Brian Clark, *How to Use the "Rule of Three" to Create Engaging Content*, COPYBLOGGER, http://www.copyblogger.com/rule-of-three/ (last visited March 16, 2011).

Let's face it, something just feels right about information broken down into groups of three. Because we're used to processing information in threes, we readily accept new information presented in threes. When information is delivered in two parts, we are left wanting a third. If a third never comes, we react unfavorably, as if something is missing. Likewise, when there are four parts, we react unfavorably because there is too much information.

Therefore, when presenting information at trial, organize it into chunks of three. If you offer only two, the jury will feel that you left them hanging. They'll be waiting for a third. Likewise, four is one too many.

Although I'm sure you have heard it before, this classic formula works wonders to provide the perfect structure for an opening or closing. First, identify the three major points you want to communicate. Let's call them A, B, and C. Organize the points so that C has the most impact. Inform the jury that you are going to prove these points during trial—"During this trial, I will prove three things: A, B, and C"—and then explain how you will prove A, B, and C. Conclude by reminding the jury what you told them: "At the end of the trial, I will have proved A, B, and C. Because I have proved A, B, and C, we will ask you to render a verdict for Plaintiff."

In addition to presenting three topics, your presentation consists of three parts, which feels right to the jury. The next time you prepare an opening argument, try organizing it into three parts as described above.

One aspect of using segments is developing modules to utilize throughout the trial. Following are several modules I try to employ in trial and a brief explanation of each.

> *The Headline Module.* The Headline Module is a summary of your point. You orient your jurors by telling them what you're going to tell them. It boils down to your three most important points. I typically use headlines in opening, for example, when I promise the jury "I will prove three things to win the case."

> *The Context Module.* The Context Module provides background information needed to understand or appreciate your headline. Usually the Context Module is brief and has to do with the general background of the case. For example, you explain the financing of a real estate development project in a commercial case or the patient's general physical condition prior to the surgery in a medical malprac-

tice case. The context can be inserted at any point in the opening. It does not have to come at the beginning, though it might. You can also break up the Context Module and use it in different spots as needed to strengthen your points.

> *The Proof Module.* Points support and explain your headline. They are subheadlines that offer depth and detail. They come in three main forms: facts, analogies, and anecdotes. And you should develop your points into groupings of threes. For example, you might say the following in your Proof Module supporting the headline that Mr. Jones was in Chicago:

> We will use three types of evidence to prove that Mr. Jones was in Chicago for the meeting. First, I will show you his credit card records showing charges in Chicago. Second, I will offer into evidence the deposition testimony of the night manager at the Hilton Chicago who will tell you that a Mr. Jones was registered at the hotel on the night in question. And, finally, we will offer testimony from Mr. Smith, who says he saw Mr. Jones at the Chase Bank Building in Chicago.

If you use more than three supporting points, especially in the opening, the jury will be hard-pressed to remember them all. If you use fewer than three, your support will sound skimpy. Think about it: we have all heard that good things come in threes.

> *The Facts Module.* Facts can be financial or other metrics, accolades from third parties, survey results, polling data, or outcomes of a study. Especially handy are facts that lend themselves to visual imagery. Facts are absolutely necessary for credibility, but don't make the mistake of piling fact upon fact. Keep them in digestible and memorable groups of three. Be sure to shuffle your facts with analogies and anecdotes.

> *The Analogies Module.* Analogies create comparisons that relate your key points to similar scenarios in the juror's real-world experience. These work best and are easily applied in the opening or closing. For example, I have used analogies to parenting, athletic events, and well-known historical events or cultural concepts that everyone understands and accepts. In a fraud case, my client had been deceived in the purchase of a sale of a security. In closing I used the refrain of "Don't buy what the defendant is selling" to analo-

gize how we had been deceived to what would happen if the jury believed the story being told by the defendant.

> *The Anecdotes Module.* Anecdotes are stories or concrete examples of your message points. Most of us remember a good story better than any other kind of content.

> *The Sound Bites Module.* Sound bites are short, catchy refrains that resonate in the listener's mind and that ring truer as you build your case. They are the calling card of Evangelical preachers ("Praise the Lord!" or "Can I get an Amen?"), but they can be appropriated by anyone who wants his message to resonate. Who can forget the late Johnnie Cochran's signpost in the O.J. Simpson trial, "If it doesn't fit, you must acquit!" One caveat, though: Use signposts sparingly, as they can easily be overdone or sound corny.

> *The Summary Module.* Here you tell the jury what you told them. You briefly summarize your message. Your summary should leave no doubt in the jurors' minds as to what you want their takeaway to be.

> *The Call-to-Action Module.* In the Call-to-Action Module, you tell your jurors what you want them to do with the information. Why are we in this courtroom in the first place? We want them to reach a verdict in favor of our clients. You would be amazed at how many trial lawyers complete their opening without telling jurors what they are supposed to do at the end of the trial. Or their closing without going through the jury charge and telling the jury how you are asking them to complete the verdict form. Whether to choose "yes" or "no" might seem obvious to you, the trial lawyer, but it is often not so obvious to jurors or easy for them to connect the dots. A clear call for action remedies this confusion. These calls are compelling, energizing requests that you make of the jury, explaining what action they should take at the end of the trial.

2. What's Your Headline?

On the news in any town in America, the anchorperson briefly greets viewers and then delivers the headlines, usually one-line summaries of the three top stories. These headlines, or "teasers," are offered up front with good reason: They let people know what information, out of all the possible stories, is considered to be the most important or interesting right now.

A clear, concise headline delivered with an intriguing hook will entice viewers to hold on for the full story. They'll stick around even if it means waiting out a toothpaste commercial, weather updates, and helicopter shots of a jackknifed tractor trailer. This is a good example of the Segmentation Principle. Tiny segments will keep the interest of a television audience. This approach piques their interest and adds to the stickiness of the headline topics. It works the same with your jury.

Have you ever gone to a restaurant and felt overwhelmed by the size and variety of the menu? I feel that way every time I go to the Cheesecake Factory. They have this huge menu with a large variety of choices on it. In fact, there is so much to choose from that it's hard for me to decide what I want. In fact, I don't really go there anymore. Don't offer a Cheesecake Factory–sized menu to your jury. Think of your trial presentation as the menu at your favorite bistro—with a few select dishes, so your diners will have no choice but to select quality. You need to know what is most important. What will be the focus of your menu? Tell your audience what they should focus on and what they should remember. You can do this with headlines. Headlines tell your jury what you're going to tell them, but that's not all: headlines also have to give your jurors a reason to stay tuned.

Now, you know what goes into a headline. But it's also important to know what to leave out. Remember, people's brains are overcrowded. In order for them to stick with you after the headline, that headline has to be free of language that weighs it down. So at all costs, avoid the following:

> Overly complex words: Is your headline: "My client's paradigm was clouded in his munificent endowment by the allure of Miss Jones's pulchritude"? Well, good luck with that. But you'd probably do better to craft your headline in plain English: "My client's opinion of the donation was clouded by the charms of Miss Jones."

> Insider terms: Don't use legalese. Your jury will be left in the dark and, worse, you'll be seen as pompous and you'll lose the jury.

Once you have your headline, you can use it to structure the remainder of your message modules. The first thing you want to do is reinforce your headline with three message points designed to support your client's case. The three points have to be repeated. That doesn't mean repeating them verbatim like a broken record or scratched CD. Repetition is achieved by expressing those three points in three different ways.

For each point, look for a metric or a quote from an outside party (your Facts Module), a colorful comparison (your Analogies Module), or an engaging story or specific example (your Anecdotes Module). Expressing your points in this variety of ways ensures that your ideas will resonate with different types of people. Organize the presentation of each point so that you can ease the audience into the flow and end it crisply.

While organizing, don't forget "chunking," or breaking down large chunks of information into more manageable pieces. Recently I saw a video about world change. It started out by discussing the world's population, which is over 6.76 billion people. Of course, this number is too large for someone to comprehend. Can you picture 6.76 billion of anything? To make 6.76 billion people more digestible, the video creator took away the number 6.76 billion, and in its place, used 100 for 100 percent. The message—100 percent change—became clear. The mind-blowingly large number became easier to comprehend when expressed as a percentage.

Whenever you're presenting a case that involves numbers, the jurors will find it hard to process steps and totals in their minds. To assist them, break the numbers down for them and then come back to the original number. With this step-by-step process, you will capture their attention and serve the jury bite-sized pieces for easier digestion.

Following are a few more suggested guidelines for building jury presentations that communicate your message effectively, starting with preparing to speak to your jury. My advice is to aim for the middle range (what I define as a high school grade), and include some information specifically aimed at the less educated and higher educated. Avoid catering to the lowest common denominator, which will be too simplistic and bore most of the jury. Also, do you remember your school days? There is a reason that your elementary teachers had show-and-tell. Different parts of the brain deal with language and vision, and we humans host the two channels for receiving visual and audio information for memory separately. When you present information both visually and audibly, you have two chances to get that material into the memory banks of your audience's mind. So combine graphics and text whenever possible to help the jury remember what you're saying. Seeing a variety of visuals will keep your audience's interest and attention. Video clips can be even more effective, because of the added dimension of movement and sound.

Planning is just as important as practice. Plan in advance how you will captivate the jury's attention. Controlling what the jury looks at and listens to will maximize the chances that they will follow you. One rule of thumb is that each slide should contain no more than six words. If you present too much text or too many graphics, the jurors will lock onto one form of communication and tune out the other. Also, every slide must reinforce your presentation and be perceptually distinct. Your very first slide should define the topic and set the stage for your presentation.

As part of the introduction, you should state up front and briefly what your conclusion will be and how you will get there. Prepare slides, and practice what you will say about each slide and your transition. Smooth transitions will keep the audience interested, and you won't have to wonder how you will get from one slide to the next. You will have a road map and so will the jury.

Capture the audience's attention by making important elements larger, brighter, or louder so that you control what the audience members pay attention to. How you highlight your material should depend on the type of material you are highlighting. If you want the jury to understand a complex structure for an organizational chart, it makes sense to build up a slide one part at a time, only showing the part you want to talk about at that moment. If you simply want to focus on a specific part, it makes sense to build a pointer into your slide by including a red arrow that points to the subject of interest, or a circle around a portion of the graphics or text that is your focus. Don't lose your basic message by providing either too much or too little information.

Don't forget to keep your eye on the ball. Remember what message you want to communicate and what you want the jurors to take away with them when they leave the courtroom. Tell the jury what you want them to conclude. Provide no more and no less information than is needed to accomplish this goal. The usual temptation is to provide more information than is necessary to make your point, which is not a good idea for at least two reasons: by forcing the jury to search for what is important, you prevent them from devoting their full resources to process what is important; also, you may push the jury to the point that they simply tune you out.

To keep your jurors from becoming overwhelmed, leave out irrelevant detail. Be careful not to discard crucial aspects of your case. Cut to the bone, but not into it.

As you've learned in this chapter, an effective presentation has a clear structure. When each part has a distinct focus, it clearly relates to the other parts. Think of the overall structure of your presentation as a pair of bookends supporting a set of books. The first bookend is the introduction. The books themselves are the body of the presentation. The final bookend is the conclusion. One fact about human memory is that we rarely remember what comes between the beginning and the ending of a speech. Therefore, the beginning and the end of your presentation are particularly important. So start with a bang. A newly elected president of the United States may have a 100-day honeymoon after taking office, but on day 101, changes, implementations, and action are expected to take place. As an attorney, you're lucky if your "honeymoon" period is longer than five minutes, during which time the jury is willing to give you the benefit of the doubt and listen. If during this period you don't grab their attention and convince them that you have something of value to say, they will be lost to you.

If the structure of your argument involves making distinct points or addressing a set of related topics, avoid making your presentation one long string. Organize it into digestible modules and give the audience a conceptual structure of the major parts of your presentation so they can anticipate what you're going to say. Ensure that the transitions between parts are clear. Organize the parts so that each provides the foundation for the next.

Let them see the outline. The outline is a good way to provide conceptual structure and clarity to your presentation. Organize your outline to reduce the load on your audience members' mental process as much as possible. Presentation marches on, over time; it's not like a written oracle or report that allows the reader to set his own pace and go backwards. You need to help your audience follow along so they don't get lost, confused, or overwhelmed.

After you present the outline of the major parts of your presentation, briefly explain what is in each part. Tell a story. The human brain automatically tries to organize and make sense out of experience. One happy consequence of this tendency is that humans like to know and understand stories. In your story, create a clear line of argument from the beginning to the end. Along the way, you build the case for the conclusion or conclusions you want the jury to draw. Provide concrete, specific evidence to support your conclusions. As I stressed, you must decide what message you want the jury members to take away from the presentation as a whole, and you must do the same thing for each part. Think of the story and how it unfolds. Only then can you know how to present clear specific evidence to back up your message. Conclude each part in support with a summary. Even if the audience doesn't follow every word, a summary at the end of each part will give them the basis of your presentation.

Another way to ensure that the jury follows along is to prepare demonstrations. People automatically pay attention to sudden change. There is nothing more engaging than a change from boring Q&A to a show-and-tell demonstration. Plus, as you know, actively processing information helps people understand and remember. To keep your audience alert and engaged, prepare a demonstration and make eye contact at every opportunity.

3. Preparing the Wrap-up

As you've learned, presentations—whether opening or closing—begin with your explaining to the audience what you're going to tell them, then continue with your telling it to them, and finally wrap up with your reminding them what you just told them. Because people best remember the beginning and the end of a sequence, the end of the presentation is very important. Here are four recommendations for the all-important wrap-up segment of your presentation:

> First, remind the jury of your key points in your opening statement.
> Next, use text and graphics to emphasize your conclusions. For the opening, ask yourself: If your jury were to give a one- or two-sentence summary of your case to a friend, what would it be? In the closing, use the jury change and write in the answers.
> Instead of trusting memory, come prepared to make your crucial points. One way to give your audience the message directly is to return to the same graphics that you showed in the introduction, but

now add some text or verbal explanation to help your audience see them in a new light.

> Finally, set up a snappy ending, and you should close crisply and be satisfied that you've put in place the final bookend. I can't count the number of times I've heard lengthy presentations that end with a statement such as "Well, that's it" or "Okay, that's all I want to say," leaving the audience wondering whether or not the statement has ended. When appropriate, an effective way to end is by using a well-chosen image.

In the words of James Roosevelt: "My father gave me these hints on speech making: 'Be sincere . . . be brief . . . and be seated.'" Yet another example of the power of three.

CHAPTER 10

The Multimedia Principle: People Learn Better from Words and Pictures than from Words Alone

"If you think you're too small to be effective,
you have never been in bed with a mosquito."
—*Betty Reese, American officer and pilot*

I've captured your attention, haven't I? Admit it! You were just visualizing yourself in bed with a mosquito. If your answer is "Yes," then I've successfully incorporated the multimedia principle into this book by creating an image in your mind, without using any actual images.

At trial, if I reach the part of my jurors' brains that converts ideas to images, I've considerably increased both their understanding of the issues and the likelihood of retention. Graphics and slide shows are the most widely used tools to reach this level of understanding. As you learned in chapter 3, mixing pictures with words reaches both sides of the brain. However, caution must be taken to ensure that the images and slides you use promote the key points of the presentation and do not take away from them.

Demonstratives have both benefits and drawbacks, both of which are detailed throughout this chapter. When used properly, they facilitate multisensory learning. They can provide context, background, definitions, summaries, and so on. Complex ideas can be simplified with graphs and charts, and series of events can be summarized and relationships demonstrated with time lines. Best of all, demonstratives—good demonstratives—maintain juror attention and prevent boredom.

But demonstratives are not without their drawbacks. Bad ones can be distracting and shift the focus from important points, or worse—they can confuse the jury. Because of these drawbacks, you should carefully weigh every decision you make about demonstratives, including the first one: Do I use this demonstrative or not? If you can't easily and convincingly answer the question "Why am I creating this PowerPoint?" then you shouldn't be creating it.

On the other hand, if you decide to use demonstratives, you must do it right. Consider what type of demonstrative you are going to use—is the information complex enough to warrant a PowerPoint presentation or can you get away with using a whiteboard? Is it something you want to make permanent or just use in passing? Is it so important to your case that you want to get it admitted into evidence? Dedicate the time and thought to resolving these questions before the trial starts.

You also need to keep any technical constraints in mind. Some courthouses are not fully equipped to handle complex presentations. Even if they are, you could run into technical difficulties before or during your presentation. So before you prepare a complex series of slides, I suggest you do a few things. First, scout the actual courtroom you will be trying the case in. While you are there, ask the bailiff or the court reporter about what is possible and how reliable the equipment is. In baseball, pitchers do not start the game without inspecting the mound, analyzing the weather, and warming up. You should do the equivalent. And always have a Plan B. Otherwise, you may find yourself fiddling with the equipment while the jury gets increasingly frustrated.

The rest of this chapter discusses demonstratives in more detail and provides tips on the most effective ways to use them. The first three sections speak more broadly to all types of demonstratives, while each of the last three sections tackles a specific type. By the end of this chapter, you should be able to answer two questions: Is a multisensory presentation right for your case? If so, what type will be the most effective?

1. Less Is More

Think about a time when you were in the audience at a presentation and what you saw didn't work—and I do not mean technically; I mean you just couldn't follow the images. What was the problem? The most common answers I hear: "The graphics were cluttered"; "The words were too small to read"; "There was too much on the slide"; "The slide looked like an eye chart"; "The slide was outdated."

Step away from the lens and take the point of view of an audience member or consumer of the presentation. Ask yourself: "If I were a consumer of this presentation, what effect would it have on me? Would it make sense? Would it bore me? Would it make me think the presenter knew what he was doing? Will this presentation trigger Juror Overload?" It's imperative that you view your presentation from the perspective of a consumer of the information. If you are consuming a presentation, the two most important aspects are whether the information communicated is clear and logical and whether the presenter is reliable.

The most common problem presenters face when using graphics is that they use documents that have been submitted into evidence. The document will have an overwhelming amount of data—the text will be too small, the data will be too detailed, and the information will be contained in elaborate tables, charts, and graphs. How are jurors supposed to understand what's being shown to them on a screen when they can't even see the minutiae of what they're being shown?

What's more, lawyers frequently publish exhibits to their jury before they begin. Then the jury tries to simultaneously read the exhibit, look at the slide that the lawyer is showing, and listen to the lawyer read what's on the slide. This is known as triple delivery, and it is an all-out sensory assault on the jurors. They cannot process all the different ways they are being bombarded with information, and the quick onset of a lethal case of juror overload is guaranteed. This is but one common example of juror overload. There are three others: (1) using the slides as notes to help the presenter remember what to say; (2) cramming words, clip art, and charts onto a slide, and (3) filling every slide with extraneous information, such as a courthouse backdrop or your firm's name. Keep in mind that a presentation is a presentation, and only a presentation. It is not a document. It should reinforce the message that you, the trial lawyer, are presenting at that exact moment. Perhaps you can get a slide or two admitted as a demonstrative, but the jury cannot revisit the entire presentation at their leisure.

Even when the presentation doesn't contain too much information, it can still be distracting. When the slides go up, jurors immediately and involuntarily focus on the graphics and start to read them. When a juror engages his brain to read a slide, he also disengages the listening portion of his brain. Human beings can listen or read; they cannot do both.

Therefore, the words on the screen take center stage and the trial lawyer becomes a distant noise sounding something like the teacher in a
Charlie Brown cartoon. This problem is compounded if the trial lawyer
himself begins to read from the slide, creating a phenomenon I call "trial
karaoke" in which the lawyer stands before the jury and reads the slide.
This style of presentation is both wholly unpersuasive and incredibly
boring. The best trial presentations are those that grab the jury's attention and keep it. Your goal is to keep the jury listening to you.

Remember also that demonstratives should leverage (not replace)
your argument or your witness's testimony. That is, the jury's focus should
be on the speaker, not the slides. A master of this approach can be found
in the business world in Steve Jobs and his new product introduction for
Apple Inc. If you have not had the pleasure of watching a Steve Jobs presentation, take a few minutes to do so next time you're in front of a computer (a quick search of "Steve Jobs Presentation" will return thousands
of hits). As you watch, you'll note that the majority of his slides contain
only a small amount of information or graphics. Each slide then provides
context for a segment of his presentation—a picture of a product with the
caption "4M sold" or a pie chart with just two slices bearing the title "Market Share." With this technique, the audience sees and visually processes
the information on the slide quickly, which frees up their brains to refocus
on the presenter. The slide serves as a launching point and backdrop for
the presenter—not a replacement of the presenter.

Another pitfall is getting carried away with the bells and whistles
that presentation software makes available. Microsoft PowerPoint and
similar programs come prepackaged with all sorts of special effects. You
can slide text in, pop it up, flip it over, bounce it across, fade it out, and
swirl it around. You can even add sound effects—your bells and whistles can have bells and whistles. But this distracting madness must stop.
Such effects only detract from your presentation rather than enhance it.
These types of distractions just give the jurors an excuse to start wondering about something unimportant, such as what special effect you're
going to use next or how long it took you to make these slides. To keep
the jury's attention, your slides should be simple and your animation
nonexistent.

When putting together a PowerPoint to support your opening or
closing statement, I suggest organizing your slides with a goal of one
point per slide. To prepare for my opening, I print out the presentation

three slides to a page. I like this format because it allows me to see at a glance where I will be going next. In the margin by the slide I might write a word or two about the transition I want to use between slides or a specific exhibit number or fact I want to be sure to include. I don't cram the slides with information. In fact, I work to do just the opposite. Each individual slide is used to reinforce one point with as few words as possible (usually fewer than six) and a single image. The slides then become my conceptual outline (not an outline I will read because there is simply not enough there to read). Then I practice my presentation again and again, focusing on making smooth transitions from one point to another and analyzing the logical coherence of the entire presentation. I find that this not only improves the actual slides that I use but it also forces me to perfect the logic and flow of my arguments and explanations.

To make things clear, we need a guiding principle. The principle "less is more" should be your organizing principle when creating visuals to support your trial presentations. My mantra is: When in doubt, leave it out (or break it into another slide). To capture the benefit of presentation software, use this minimalist approach. Your slide will do its job (provide a graphic for the jury and a prompt for you) but it will not overwhelm or interfere with your opening statement or closing argument to the jury. If a slide is crowded with multiple sentences and numerous bullet points, even the most accomplished lawyer will find it hard to avoid looking at and reading from the slide. When you read your slides word for word, you abdicate your role as the advocate and assume the lowly role of reader. And everyone on that jury can read, so why should they listen to you? Courtroom karaoke is instant death for your jury's attention. Don't read the slides. People want to hear your argument, your description, and your thoughts; they do not want a recitation from the slide. Occasionally, you should try previewing—that is, introducing a slide before showing it—by asking a question such as "So what do you think that did to the defendant's sales? Up how much?" This technique is commonly used in the news media. It is called a teaser. It is used to grab your attention and make sure you are still there to hear the answer after the commercial break. It is used to hold viewer attention. It works in the courtroom as well.

To maintain attention, I generally estimate an average of one to two minutes per slide (some slides will require a bit more time, some less). That's about 15 slides for a 20-minute opening or 40 for an hour, leaving time for your introduction and summary. The less experience you have, the fewer slides you should use. In my observations, lawyers try to use too many slides in their opening and closing and end up going entirely too fast in a rush to get to all of the slides. Keep purifying your argument/slides to your most salient points. Aim for one point per slide and a maximum of six words per slide. Avoid complete sentences. The audience should literally look to you for elaboration. As Mozart said, "The silence between the notes is as important as the notes themselves." Think about it this way. In the opening, all the jury wants is for you to preview what they will see in the trial. And in the closing (after a week or two of trial), they want a summary review of the important facts and an explanation of how your arguments and facts answer the questions they will face in the jury charge. You will find that this purifying process helps you give a smoother opening or closing as well.

2. Polish Your Text

When incorporating text into your slides, follow these simple rules of thumb:

> Use a large font size. I recommend a 40-point font or larger. This keeps you from packing too much information into the slide and makes the text easier to read. You know you have too much information when PowerPoint automatically resizes your text to make it fit.

> Use a font that's easy to read. Avoid cursive fonts, highly graphical fonts, and fonts with pronounced serifs.

> Limit the word count. A large font size will usually take care of this problem, but just in case it doesn't, a good rule of thumb is no more than six words per slide.

> Limit hierarchy to three levels. Although outline format is often useful in presentations, it can be overdone. If your outline has too many levels, it will be easy for the jury to get lost in the hierarchy. Here, no point in your outline should have more than six words.

> Use effective color combinations and contrasts. Neutral colors (grays and browns) and cool colors (blues and greens) are easiest on the eyes. Warm colors (reds and oranges) are jarring and distracting. Use them to make strong points. Also, use a contrast scheme that is easy

to read—dark on light or light on dark. I like a black background with yellow lettering.

> Avoid clutter—eliminate all firm logos. They do not help you make a point with the jury and serve only to distract from what you are trying to communicate. Just as a well-placed pause in an oral presentation adds emphasis to a point, a slide with just one word and a lot of blank space around it sends a powerful message.

Horace (65–8 B.C.E.) said, "The mind is more slowly stirred by the ear than by the eye." We say, "A good picture is worth a thousand words." Although these two phrases are from different centuries, their overall meaning is generally the same: visuals are powerful. Studies have been conducted that validate this assertion. They show that 80 percent of what we learn comes to us visually[1] and that visuals double the length of time we remember things. It's been shown that words with pictures are six times more effective than words alone.[2]

3. The Power of Props

Remember your favorite science classes in school? The most memorable days were the ones where the teacher made hard-boiled eggs turn purple or created one of those vinegar-and-baking-soda volcanoes. Props! That was the ticket. Props also used to be popular in business presentations, but with the rise of PowerPoint and digital pictures, they started to vanish. Now they're beginning to make a comeback. At first you might feel silly using props. Isn't that for imitation magicians who pull rabbits out of top hats? Even though this practice might not be in your comfort zone, it works. Props are a way to move the needle and grab or keep attention.

Who can forget Colin Powell holding a model while giving a presentation to the UN Security Council, or Tim Russert on election night with his little handheld eraser board and marker demonstrating the change in the senate majority or electoral college predictions? Both of these individuals used props to grab and keep the attention of their audience, while at the same time reinforcing their message.

1 http://www.child-control.com/learning-styles-children.htm.
2. M. A. Cohena et al., *Auditory Recognition Memory Is Inferior to Visual Recognition Memory*, 106 PROC. NAT'L ACAD. SCI. 6008–10 n.14 (2009).

I have spent most of my words on what to do. Let's change gears and allow me to give you some advice on what to *stop* doing. Lose your laser pointer. Unless you have a "very steady hand," as they used to say in the commercial for the game Operation, a laser pointer is a distracting prop. Your presentation turns into a game of "follow the bouncing ball." Jurors find that jiggling red dot both irritating and distracting. If you must point to something, walk up to it and point to it. Be sure that you are not speaking as you face away from the jury, because they will not hear you. And if you find that your hand shakes when you do that, use the move patented by Vanna White and use your open palm to identify what you want. The small muscles in you finger and hands are what cause the shakes. If you use your entire arm to move your palm, you are using larger muscles and should eliminate all of the shaking caused by nerves.

No matter which type of aid you use, remember that demonstratives are only aids to increase the jury's comprehension, not a substitute for a well-planned presentation. There is no more powerful impeachment than to ask a witness on the stand a question like "Where were you at 2:00 p.m. on June 13, 2008?" Have his live answer be that he was at his office in Dallas, Texas. And then play a video clip from his deposition where you asked the witness the exact same question and the jury sees and hears the witness answer, "I was in Chicago for a meeting with Acme." The video brings the answer to life and makes the point that this witness is lying in a way that simple reading cannot.

4. Boardwork

Think of the worst professor you ever had. Can you picture him, his back to you, mumbling something no one can hear and writing something no one can read on the board? And what he writes probably isn't all that helpful in the first place—it's just a random string of words and phrases with no context. Maybe some words are circled, others underlined, and there are random arrows connecting certain phrases to each other in confusing ways. If there happens to be anything important on the board, it's written so small that you have to strain to read it. At the end of class, the board is filled with a bunch of gobbledygook that nobody, including the professor, can make any sense of. These are the dangers of bad boardwork.

If you are going to use a whiteboard or chalkboard at trial, plan ahead. It is best to know not only *what* you are going to write, but also *when* in your presentation you will write it. Use these pointers in your planning:

> **Prepare.** Do a couple of run-throughs of your presentation so you get comfortable with writing on the board.

> **Focus.** Don't talk when you're writing and don't write when you're talking. If you do, you will inevitably misspell or omit a word. The last thing you need at trial is twelve people staring at the word "exihbit" or "neligence," wondering when you will catch the mistake and fix it.

> **Print.** Do not write in cursive. It has too much of a tendency to become illegible, especially if you are trying to write quickly.

> **Abbreviate.** Avoid writing long, convoluted sentences. Sum up your ideas in a few short words in bullet-point format.

> **Right size.** Write large enough that the jury can read, but not so large that you have to erase and start over.

> **Talk to the jury.** Whenever you say something, turn all the way around and face the jury. Don't talk to the board.

> **Write high.** Consider where the jury is sitting and whether they can all see what you're writing. Don't write so low on the board that the jurors in the back row have to move around to see.

> **Cap markers.** If you use multiple colored markers, cap each one after you use it. You don't want six uncapped markers creating a cloud of toxic fumes near the board. Also, uncapped markers tend to dry out quickly, making them unusable.

5. Flip Charts

Though I am a fan of PowerPoint, visuals don't have to be high-tech to make a lasting impression. Research shows that people remember items such as bar graphs or bell curves on flip charts longer than they remember computer-generated graphics. The act of watching the presenter create data in real time is engaging.

When using flip charts, it's a good idea to sketch information such as numbers in light pencil before presenting. Just as with chalkboards or whiteboards, be sure not to talk and write at the same time or turn your back on the jury while talking, because you won't project well and you'll lose all-important eye contact. Always turn to talk to your audience. If you're right-handed, the flip chart should be on your left. Point to information with your left hand, palm open. If you feel uncomfortable giving up your notes to use the flip chart, you can use a piece of paper to map out the points you want to make on the flip chart.

Many of the same points under the boardwork section above apply here as well. You want to keep each page uncluttered and legible, so write big and limit each chart to one or two main ideas. Also, when you talk, take a step away from the chart so everyone on the jury can see it.

There are, however, a few differences between flip charts and chalkboards or whiteboards. For example, you have to flip the pages on the easel as you go, so it may be useful to create tabs for each page. Also, flip charts can be prepared in advance. But if you do this, make sure you time each page properly. You don't want to turn to a prepared page prematurely, because the jury will stop focusing on you and start reading what's on the flip chart.

If you decide not to prepare the flip chart in advance, you have to be much more careful because you can't easily erase a flip chart. A good way around this problem is again to lightly pencil in what you're going to put on the flip chart ahead of time. You can do this in one of two ways—either write small notes to yourself on the chart so you know what to put on the chart or just create the whole chart beforehand in very light pencil so you can trace over it with a marker at trial. In either case, test out your prepared flip chart to make sure the jurors can't see your prepared work.

6. Overheads

An overhead projector, or Elmo, is common in courts that have not yet fully upgraded their audiovisual technology. Overheads are beneficial in that they are easy to prepare, inexpensive, and reusable. Additionally, they share some qualities with both PowerPoint presentations and whiteboards. As in PowerPoint presentations, you can prepare a series of overhead laminates and treat them like slides. And as with a whiteboard or a flip chart, you can write on these overheads as you advance your presentation. But be careful—many of the previously described pitfalls apply here as well. Thus, try to keep the following points in mind when choosing overheads for your multimedia presentation.

> Create paper copies of your entire set of overheads. As you practice your presentation, write notes on the paper copies. This way, when you go through each overhead, you will have your notes handy without having to write them on the actual overhead in advance.

> Adjust and focus the overhead projector prior to trial. Many courtrooms will have all of this taken care of, but take the time to find out for yourself. Make sure that the projected image is completely within the screen area and that the projector itself is not in the way.

> Don't stand by the projector throughout the presentation. Practice moving away from it and talking about each overhead from the same place you would as if it were not on. Even when you're switching overheads or writing on one, face the audience.

> If you only need it for small segments of your presentation, turn the projector off when you're not using it. You don't want an overhead to linger as you move way past it in your presentation.

> Watch the size of your overheads. Some projectors have a small projecting surface, so your audience may not be able to see the entire overhead.

> Limit the number of overheads. Just like slides, each overhead should be up for no more than a few minutes. So in a fifteen-minute presentation, you would have five to seven overheads.

> Just as with slides, create a roadmap overhead that you can refer to every so often, especially if your presentation is going to be long. After every section, you can put the same overhead back up and even cross out or check off the items you've discussed.

> Declutter your overheads. Limit the amount of information on each overhead—each one should be legible and easy to follow.

> Remember that overheads can be layered for added effect. For example, if you have a bare map on one overhead, you can place another one over it that contains a series of marks that designate trees. Then you can place another overhead over those two that contains some structures such as buildings and fences. A fourth layer can be added that depicts where various people were located at a certain time.

> At the end of the presentation, either return to your roadmap over-
> head or introduce a summary overhead that describes what you've
> talked about.

In conclusion, whatever tool you decide to use when delivering a
multimedia presentation, remember that it is a tool, not the presenter.
The focus should always be on you.

CHAPTER 11

The Coherence (Less-Is-More) Principle: People Learn Better When Extraneous Material Is Excluded

> "Make sure you have finished speaking before
> your audience has finished listening."
> —*Dorothy Sarnoff, Broadway singer and author*

As discussed in chapter 4, the coherence principle has two main aspects. First, the trial presentation must be built with the end or jury charge in mind. Every aspect of the trial should be relevant to what you want your jury to know and conclude when they walk into the jury room to deliberate. Second, the jury should be told exactly what they must know to reach your verdict: telling them too little will leave them puzzled, and telling them too much will leave them overwhelmed, disoriented, and irritated. Effective communication in the courtroom is based on grabbing the jury's attention and keeping it focused on your best facts and themes.

When I first began trying cases, I thought that the goal was to convey as much information on a topic as possible—and I utterly failed to connect with the members of the jury. I would rush through summaries and examples, swamping the jurors in massive amounts of information, talk, and exhibits. The problem, I found, was that I was talking for myself, not the members of the jury. I now view that as a complete failure; after all, I already knew what I had to say. The only people that mattered were the 12 individuals in the jury box. I had to learn to speak to the jury with the intent to educate rather than speak at them with the intent to impress.

For example, you probably know that the Gettysburg Address was short. But perhaps you don't know exactly how short. It was 10 sentences—a mere 272 words—and took two minutes to deliver start to finish. This is another fine example of the "less is more" aspect of communication. As Mark Twain stated, "The difference between the right word and the almost right word is the difference between lightning and a lightning bug." Focus your message and eliminate all nonessential aspects of the case. Choose words that will have the largest impact. This is something I'd like to see in every courtroom throughout America. Can you imagine the wasted time that would be regained if every trial attorney honed this skill? If I ruled the courtrooms of the world, I would limit opening or closing to 20 minutes. You really do not need more than that to summarize a trial of a week or two.

1. Curse of Knowledge

One of the greatest challenges that face trial lawyers as we prepare for trial is how to explain the case. It is a problem to challenge even Goldilocks and her legendary knack for getting it "just right." In our opening, we do not want to say too much and bore our jury, but at the same time we do not want to leave out key points and lose our jury. For many lawyers, when the time for trial arrives, their intense involvement and huge history in the case hinders their ability to focus their message and get it "just right." They present the case as though every fact is vital and every event in a time line indispensable. They can't see the forest for the trees. In order to avoid this mistake, you have to be able to tease out the crucial facts and present only those to the jury.

Recall from earlier chapters that your trial goals are to educate the jury about your facts, convince them that your theory of the case is true, and make them empathize with your client. When you meet these goals, you have incited the jury to act—to return a verdict in your favor. Their action, then, is based on their belief that your client deserves to win, which turns on their belief that what you told them is true. Therefore, if a particular fact does not advance one of these goals, you don't need it. And you need to be ruthless in applying this analysis to your efforts.

As I have suggested throughout the pages of this book, there are a multitude of causes, effects, and actions that break, disrupt, or destroy your connection with the jury. Face it—for better or worse, we are a society whose attention span shrinks with each passing year. The management at network and cable news organizations measures the rate at which audiences slip off—that is, how many viewers stop watching a broadcast. Every morning, news anchors are handed a Nielsen report capturing minute by minute the audience shrink from the previous day's broadcast. In today's environment, trial lawyers need to take a page out of the broadcast news playbook and find methods and techniques to maintain a high level of attention from juries. Trial presentations, like newscasts, need to be choreographed (with a beginning, middle, and end) to attract and maintain attention. In order to accomplish this, you'll need to do three things: (1) cut to the chase; (2) jolt, so they don't bolt; and (3) keep yourself on a tight time clock.

A listener's attention is often high at the start of your opening, so make sure you start with a bang. It's really important that you cut to the chase at the beginning. The jury is dying to learn why they are there and what they will be spending their time trying to resolve. So give it to them right up front. Don't make them wait. One way to achieve this is to use your headlines. Whatever you do, don't bury that headline or dawdle along the path to it. Be aware that time is of the essence. And above all, grab them from the start. For example, in most of my openings I dispense with all of the warm-up preamble mumbo-jumbo and go straight to the meat of the case. I tell the jury: "During the course of this trial, I will prove three things. . . ." I then identify the three most important facts (for me to prevail) in the entire case. I usually follow that with "Once I prove these three facts, you will be able to use these three facts to answer every question in the jury charge." I want the jury to know right up front where this case is going and how we will get there.

I continue to use headlines and road maps at the start of examination to take advantage of primacy, the concept that we remember best that which comes first. When a new witness comes on the stand, I try to create a headline for that witness. After the witness has stated his name for the jury, I will ask, "Why are you here today?" The answer that I'm looking for is something like "I am an accounting expert and here to explain why the accounting presented by XYZ Company was not reliable." Or "I am an employee of Acme Company and was on watch during the night of the plant explosion." I want to orient the jury as to who this witness is and where he fits into the case from the very start. As a result of the answer to this headline question, the jury immediately knows who this witness is and what the point of his testimony will be. It also sets the stage and tells the jury what it should be listening for during the course of this witness's testimony.

In the *Family Circus* cartoon, when we follow the dotted line as little Billy twists, turns, and meanders through the neighborhood to avoid going home for bath time, we find it cute and amusing. At trial a twisting and meandering path to your destination is neither cute nor amusing. It is most likely going to cause you to lose your traveling companions along the way. In addition, you are sending a clear message about what you think of their time: namely, that their time isn't of value to you. For each of us, our time is valuable. Once gone, we can't wish or buy it back. Think about how you feel when someone else squanders your time. Think of the guy in the "10 items" line who has 15 items, the customer service phone rep who consigns you to music limbo, and the cable repairman who says he'll be there between 8 and 12 and shows up at 3. Now try that shoe on the other foot and imagine being the guilty party. Do you think anyone will harbor warm feelings for you, the source of the delay, or your client? Remember the golden rule of trial presentation: don't waste for others that which you wouldn't waste for yourself.

Some of the best thinking and teaching on how cutting to the chase increases coherence can be found in *The Laws of Simplicity* by John Maeda.[1] I recommend it to you, but let me give you a brief summary here to whet your appetite. The book contains 10 chapters, each pronouncing a different "law" of simplicity. For example, he demonstrates how reduction, organization, and context can be used to simplify a presentation and communicate a message more effectively. Following his own advice, Maeda limited the book to a hundred pages, making it an easy read.

In one way or another, the advice in Maeda's book is covered here as well. In the chapters about ethos, for example, I discussed how to make the jury empathize with you and your client—an idea Maeda touches on in his chapter titled "Emotion." Maeda's book focuses on simplicity as an end in itself, but most of his theories and ideas can be applied by you and me in the courtroom to make our message to the jury simple, clear and to the point.

Invoking *The Lord of the Rings*, Maeda calls his tenth law "the One"—the one rule to bind them all. In the final chapter, Maeda says, "Simplicity is about subtracting the obvious, and adding the meaningful." This is sage advice for a trial lawyer. As mentioned above, you will have to

---

1. John Maeda, The Laws of Simplicity (2006).

discern which of your facts are crucial to your case and which ones are just noise. This is one of those skills that takes little time to learn, but a lifetime to master.

2. Keeping It Simple

Here's a riddle that teaches an important lesson to trial lawyers: "How do you eat an elephant?" The answer, "One bite at a time," should guide your case presentation strategy. Often, the message you have to convey to the jury will be quite complex. Patent cases come to mind, with all the technical data, diagrams, expert testimony, etc. But even seemingly simple cases can involve complex ideas.

Take, for example, a subrogation case. On the surface, the idea is simple—Alice injured Bob; Bob's insurance company paid for his loss; so now the insurance company has a claim against Alice. But at trial, things can get hairy. The insurer must prove that the loss was covered by Bob's policy, which Alice can of course dispute. Now, what seemed like a simple case rests on the jury wading through hundreds of pages of an insurance policy.

What's the cure for complexity? Reduction. Just about everything can be reduced to its component parts. Bob's insurance policy no doubt contains sections and paragraphs that are irrelevant to the lawsuit. And even those sections that *are* relevant can be explained by breaking them down into simple units. There's a section that talks about what the policy covers; there's a section on exclusions that talks about what the policy doesn't cover; and so on.

Reduction requires a continuing effort. Not only are you going to exclude some relatively unimportant facts from your trial, but some of the facts that you *do* introduce are going to be omitted from your closing argument. In other words, don't try to make the jury swallow the elephant whole.

In the subrogation example, imagine that during the course of the trial you put on an expert witness to talk about industry practices. The first few questions you ask him are meant to help the jury understand who he is, what he does, and why his opinion matters. To firmly ground his credibility, this may include questions about his education, his training, and his experience. Only then do you actually ask him his opinion. But when you get to your closing argument, you don't repeat all of this information. In the few minutes you can dedicate to discussing the expert's opinions, you simply don't have time to recite his entire curriculum vitae.

Going back to Maeda's book, he suggests three "keys" to simplification through reduction: away, open, and power. I think the first key is the most important—when presenting an idea, you can make it appear simpler by "moving it far, far away." Maeda uses Google as an example: When you browse to google.com, you are greeted with a very simple interface. Just type what you're looking for and Google will find it for you.

Now, whether you know it or not, there is a tremendous amount of work that goes into finding your information. There is an algorithm that compares your query to Google's index of websites, a program that returns relevant results, and web-based code that turns the results into a web page. But you don't see any of this happening because the work is done remotely. What you see is local.

There are three lessons in the Google example, one substantive, one structural, and one stylistic. The substantive lesson is that you have to do the work yourself. As discussed throughout this book, you have to be an expert in the facts and the law of your case. If you're representing either Alice or Bob in the example above, you have to know the insurance policy well enough to understand what parts of it are extraneous to your case. In other words, you must understand the complexity before you can present the simplicity.

The structural lesson is that you have to organize your case in a way that reduces the complexity. This means that you have to question the importance and relevance of every aspect of your case. For every question you formulate, exhibit you present, and argument you make, you should ask yourself these questions: Is this information important? Does it advance one of my goals? Is this the right time to present it? Is there a less confusing way to put it before the jury? Does the jury need to know something more in the way of background before this information is presented to them?

Finally, the stylistic lesson is that the whole trial should look effortless. Just like Google's interface, your presentation is the piece that connects the work you've done to the information that the jury sees. Google users generally don't care about the search engine's inner workings—users simply want it to work. They want their question answered immediately and correctly. In fact, if the result isn't what they wanted, some of them get very impatient. Rather than ask the question in a different way, they will look to other search engines, such as Yahoo or Bing, for the answer. Your problem at trial is slightly different, but the consequences are grave: the only alternative at trial is your opponent. And the last thing you want a juror to do is turn away from you and go to your opponent to get their questions answered.

These lessons highlight the point of this chapter—the jury will understand you better when you get rid of extraneous material. You facilitate their learning process by providing not only fewer facts, but also simple ones. So how do you feed an elephant to a jury? Trim the fat, and cut the remainder into bite-sized chunks. Your trial should give jurors something to chew on, and your closing argument should help them swallow and digest it.

CHAPTER 12

Stickiness Principle: How to Make an Idea Stick

"Go ahead, make my day."
—*Harry Callahan (Clint Eastwood) in* Sudden Impact

There have been words and phrases spoken throughout time that have the sticky factor we discussed earlier in the book, such as Arnold Schwarzenegger's "I'll be back" and Cuba Gooding Jr.'s "Show me the money!" Little else is remembered from the O.J. Simpson trial except for the famous line "If it doesn't fit, you must acquit." Seriously, can you recall any other words from the trial, verbatim, as you do that single phrase? It's brilliant! It illustrates that the key evidence against the defendant did not "fit" the prosecutor's case, and then it directed the jurors to act, making a decision favorable to the defense. This phrase was the Holy Grail for any defense attorney.

Thus far in this book, we've discussed different ways to persuade the jury. From Aristotle's modes of rhetoric to PowerPoint presentations and other technology, the focus has been getting the jury to believe your facts over your opponent's. But even if your presentation persuades the jury in that moment, you still need them to remember your persuasive arguments when they retire to the jury room. This is where stickiness comes in. If you can make your arguments "stick" in the jurors' minds, they'll be more likely to vote in your favor.

More importantly, sticky arguments can win the day when the jurors are split on an issue. Often you will fail to persuade the entire jury with your presentation. It might be 8 to 4 in your favor or even 1 to 11 against you.[1] But remember the film *Twelve Angry Men*—if you have convinced

---

1. In many jurisdictions, a jury does not have to be unanimous to return a verdict in civil cases. Some jurisdictions even permit a nonunanimous verdict in criminal cases. For a complete list of these rules, *see* BUREAU OF JUSTICE STATISTICS, DEP'T OF JUSTICE, REPORT ON STATE COURT ORGANIZATION, 233-37 (2004), *available at* http://bjs.ojp.usdoj.gov/content/pub/pdf/sco04.pdf.

even one juror that your case is worth arguing for, she will carry your banner into the jury room. It is then that your sticky presentation will resurface, and you'll have a second shot at convincing the jury through your advocates.

One of the best books on stickiness is *Made to Stick* by Dan and Chip Heath.[2] The brothers studied many facets of what makes ideas stay with us. Some of the ideas they examined were proverbs, urban legends, and ad campaigns—all areas in which the goal is to make others remember the idea. By the end of their research, they realized that every sticky idea has six attributes: Simplicity, Unexpectedness, Concreteness, Credibility, Emotions, and Stories ("SUCCESs"). Going further, they argue that although it might seem easy to incorporate all of these principles into an idea, we're faced with a giant barrier—the Curse of Knowledge. In this chapter, I discuss how the stickiness principles of the Heath brothers apply to a trial setting. But first, I will discuss an important issue that can impede your ability to get your sticky ideas across: the jitters.

1. The Jitters

Anyone who has tried a case can tell you that jurors get bored very quickly. It's virtually impossible to have every juror's attention for every second of trial. They get restless, lose focus, and drift away on what one presentation expert calls "journeys of self discovery."[3] In other words, if you give the jury an excuse to let their minds wander, they'll take it.

Capturing and keeping a jury's attention is much easier said than done. It requires you to be a dynamic presenter, a creative storyteller, and a credible teacher all at the same time. To juggle these roles effectively, you first have to be confident in courtroom.

Recall the courtroom scene from *My Cousin Vinny* we discussed in Chapter 6. One of the defendants decided to go with a court-appointed attorney who seemed to have everything together. There was only one problem—he was so nervous that he stammered over every sentence.

---

2. Dan Heath & Chip Heath, Made to Stick: Why Some Ideas Survive and Others Die (2d ed. 2008).
3. Douglas Jefferys, Enhancing Your Presentation Skills (2009).

Now, if you've seen the movie, chances are that you can remember his stammering and spitting on the jury, but you have no idea what he said.

It is said that of all the phobias, glossophobia (the fear of public speaking) is the most common. Noting a survey that showed this fear to be even more common than the fear of dying, Jerry Seinfeld joked that at a funeral, the person delivering the eulogy would rather be in the casket. Now, I'm guessing that glossophobia is not nearly as common in trial lawyers as it is in the general population, because many people who are terrified of public speaking self-select out of litigation roles early in their legal career. But I know quite a few attorneys who still get nervous in front of audiences.

When you're nervous, it'll show. And if that happens, your arguments will not resonate with the jury. Rather, the only thing they'll remember is your mumbled words, your shaky hands, or the bead of sweat trickling down your face. At that point, it won't matter what you say or what the merits of your case may be. Your jury will have lost confidence in you.

If you get nervous speaking in front of an audience, simply reading that last paragraph may have made your heart race a bit. So how do you get rid of your nerves? I often hear so-called experts share useless advice such as "Imagine your audience in their underwear." The point behind this is to make your audience seem weakened, disadvantaged, and different from you, the speaker. To me, this seems both silly and counterproductive.

On the silly side, imagine actually being in a room where everyone is in their underwear. If your first thought isn't "What the hell am I doing here," then you may need help. On the more serious side, advice like that undermines your ultimate goal. In any public speaking forum, your goal is to join with, rather than separate yourself from, your audience. If you're picturing them in their underwear, you are separating them from you, not embracing a connection with them.

In Chapter 6, I discussed nervousness and provided some techniques to help alleviate it. There's no need to rehash that discussion here. But what's important to the present discussion is that nervousness not only prevents you from connecting with the audience, but also removes the stickiness from your case. Ultimately, you should realize that you will get less and less nervous the more you connect with the audience. Using stories, illustrations, vignettes, and anecdotes are fantastic ways of establishing that important relationship. Good speakers are good storytellers, and audiences can relate to them in a way they won't relate to anything else.[4] In fact, storytelling is so important that it's included in the six principles of stickiness below.

2. Achieving SUCCESs

In this section, we'll discuss the Heath brothers' theory about stickiness. But first, let's return to the distinction between stickiness and persuasiveness. Earlier in this chapter, I mentioned that this book has covered many stickiness principles, but with an eye toward persuading the jury. That's still true. But notice as you read this section how the Heath brothers' stickiness principles also align with our tenets of persuasion. Once you realize that the two ideas (stickiness and persuasiveness) go hand in hand, you'll begin to see how effective your presentation can be.

A. Simplicity

It's no coincidence that the first of the stickiness principles is simplicity. It's the most important principle of stickiness. As the Heath brothers say, "[R]arely will you get advice to make your communications lengthy and convoluted, unless you write interest-rate disclosures for a credit card company." They don't expound on that simple example, but I think it's a perfect point for lawyers.

First, it shows you how the authors (and the world) view lawyers. The common misconception is that lawyers make things complicated in order to pull a fast one on others—that somehow, we have a nefarious goal of burying the truth in a mountain of words. But in reality, documents such as interest rate disclosures are complicated because they reflect decades, sometimes centuries, of litigation. A sentence is unclear, the borrower sues the lender because of it, the court resolves the ambiguity, the lender changes the disclosure to reflect the court's decision, and the industry adopts the new language to prevent further litigation. Over time, more and more language gets added until the disclosure statement

---

4. http://www.itemupon.com/article/34428/advice-Public-Relations-Primer-Part-III-10-Don-ts.html.

reads like the tax code. This isn't some evil intent on the part of lawyers; it's simply evolution over time.

Second, it gives you insight about your trial technique. You won't find any book telling you to make your trial so complicated that the jurors are confused. But this is where the Curse of Knowledge comes in. The Curse is something of a paradox. Before you know something, your lack of knowledge prevents you from effectively explaining it to others. But after you know something, your *abundance* of knowledge gives the same result. The problem with having the knowledge is that you don't remember what it was like to *not* have it. So it becomes hard for you to explain it to others in a way that makes sense.

The solution to this is to keep it simple. At trial, you want to present a theme that encompasses everything that you're trying to instill in the jury. Though they don't call it a "theme," the Heath brothers boil this principle down to a formula: "simple = core + compact." For our purposes, the word "core" refers to conveying a message that is at the heart of your case. But not only does it have to fit your case, it also has to evoke something of a universal truth. For example, you can't defend a criminal case using the theme "Rules are meant to be broken." Imagine what the prosecutor would do to that theme. Even if you're going for jury nullification, it would be better to use a theme whose core message is that the law is unfair rather than that the laws should be broken.

The word "compact" means precisely that—keep your theme short. I generally try to cut my theme down to about five to eight words. Johnny Cochran's famous theme in the O.J. Simpson trial was seven words—"If it doesn't fit, you must acquit."

The real challenge when coming up with a simple theme is when you have a complex case. This is where I depart from *Made to Stick*— the authors argue that even if you have numerous ideas to present, one of them should stand out. They use the example of Bill Clinton's 1992 presidential campaign. There, the campaign organizers were worried that Clinton's penchant for complexity would undermine the central message. Clinton's campaign people, notably James Carville, came up with the slogan "It's the economy, stupid!" and it stuck. The economy was the central theme of the Clinton campaign because it was one issue where George Bush was thought to be weak.

But a trial is different than a presidential campaign. A candidate can have a central message and can shift the focus to it in speeches and debates. That strategy is effective because voters can prioritize the issues that are important to them. But the difference between you and a candidate is that you have to prove each element of your claim or defense. Sometimes a case can be so complex that one theme can't cover all of the important issues. If you focus on one theme in these cases, your opponent will accuse you of overlooking important issues. So in these cases, I tend to use more than one theme. But remember, this is a last resort, not a first impulse. Even in the most complex cases, it's often possible to have a single, unified, overarching theme.

B. Unexpectedness

Doing the unexpected can also stick with the jury. As lawyers, we get too comfortable in our routines. This is precisely the reason that people expect us to be boring. I've heard of jurors playing "Lawyer Bingo," where they listen for common phrases from the judge or lawyers, such as "order in the court" or "beyond a reasonable doubt." When people expect you to be boring, and you shatter that expectation, you become all the more memorable. It is the unexpected that sticks with us.

This should start as early in the case as possible. When you deliver your opening, for example, start with something exciting that grabs the jurors' attention immediately. Here are some ideas:

> **Tell a story.** As discussed above, telling a story not only helps you to relax, but also draws the audience in. Example: "This is a case about three broken promises, two desperate men, and a whole lot of bad decisions."

> **Describe a current event.** Use a relevant news item as a jumping-off point to get into the facts of your case. Example: "Last Sunday, *60 Minutes* reported that over half of consumers want to know more about how corporations price their products. During this trial, you will learn about how two corporate big boys conspired to set prices in a way to eliminate smaller competition."

> **Use data or statistics.** Find survey results or data that relate to your topic. Example: "Recent survey data from National Highway Traffic Safety Administration demonstrate that four out of five people in cars today consistently wear their seat belt. If Jillian Cooper had been wearing her seat belt at 5:17 on the evening of August 23, 2010, her

death and the tragedy that you will learn about over the next few days would have been avoided."

Finally, give them a road map of what to expect. This gives the jurors something to keep track of—a checklist they can refer back to throughout the trial. This helps keep them engaged and paying attention throughout the trial. Consider the difference between these two examples:

> "I represent the Carmaker, Inc. Our main theme in the trial will be that Ms. Cooper's death could have been avoided if she had worn her seat belt on the night of the accident. We are going to talk about what Ms. Cooper could have done to avoid this tragedy and why wearing your seat belt is important."

And

> "This is a case about consequences of bad decisions. I am going to prove three things during the course of this trial. First, I will prove to you that the law requires everyone riding in a car to wear a seat belt. Second, I am going to prove to you that Jillian Cooper was not wearing her seat belt at the time of the accident. Third, I will prove, through the expert testimony of Dr. Safeland, that had Ms. Cooper been wearing her seat belt at the time of the accident, she would be sitting with us here today. At the end of the trial, we will ask you to return a verdict in favor of Carmaker Inc. because as tragic as it is, Ms. Cooper's death was the consequence of her own bad decision—the failure to wear a seat belt."

Which defense opening grabbed your attention (and gave you a step-by-step road map of the case)? Were you more intrigued by the safety-lecture style of the first or the hard-hitting detailed approach of the second? In the second example, the lawyer started off by punching the jury in the face and directly laid the blame at the feet of the victim. It's an aggressive approach, but one that he backed up with specific examples of the proof he would present at trial. Think about it: if the lawyer is convinced that winning depends on proving that Jillian Cooper was not wearing her seat belt, is there any other way to start?

C. Concreteness

For me, the most memorable part of the Concreteness chapter of *Made to Stick* was the Velcro theory of memory. The Heath brothers explained that the Velcro works because it has thousands of tiny loops on one strip and thousands of tiny hooks on another strip. When the strips are pushed together, the hooks latch on to the loops and the two strips stick together. They went on to explain that our brain contains millions of loops waiting for ideas to act as hooks. The way to make ideas stick, then, is to infuse them with hooks.

The way to do this is with concrete ideas—ideas that appeal to our senses. Consider the McDonald's hot coffee case. At trial, it is one thing to say that McDonald's coffee was served at 185°F. It is quite another to say that it caused third-degree burns after five seconds of exposure. And it is yet another thing to say that the coffee soaked her sweatpants and continued to scald her so badly that she had to be hospitalized for eight days to undergo skin-replacement surgery. These statements show three different levels of concreteness. The first is a statistic whose importance is notable only to a small number of people (e.g., fire-fighters and doctors). The second has wider appeal; we may not know exactly what a "third-degree burn" is, but we know that it's serious. The last has mass appeal. We've all experienced scalding, whether from taking a shower, washing the dishes, or cooking. So that description has an immediate impact.

There are multiple lessons here. First, statistics don't matter except when you provide context. If you present your case in the abstract, the jurors will not remember a lick of it. Second, our sensory perceptions stick with us longer than abstract ideas. Your case will stick much better when you explain it in terms of sights and sounds. And third, always use a frame of reference that a jury can understand. Your goal is to get the jurors to identify with the characters in your story, without breaking the Golden Rule (not the "do unto others" one, but the one that prohibits instructing the jury to put themselves in the victim's shoes).

Sometimes, when you ask the jury to imagine something, you'll see confused looks on their faces. When this happens, chances are that you've given them too broad a task. To show the distinction between an easy question and a hard one, the Heath brothers use these examples: First, think of five silly things that people have done over the last ten years. How many did you come up with? Now, think of five silly things that your child has done in the past week. How quickly did that list complete itself? The point is that when you try to make something concrete for the jury, you should also make it immediate. If you narrow the field of possibilities, the response will be much quicker.

D. Credibility

In earlier chapters, we discussed creditability at length. But now we're going to put a different spin on it. Whereas the focus was previously on *your* credibility, now the focus will be on the credibility of the *information* you provide. For example, compare the following pieces of information: (1) In a study, 70 percent of participants who slept on RestWell beds reported that they felt more rested the next morning; and (2) in a study, 70 percent of participants who slept on RestWell beds slept through the entire night without tossing and turning.

If you're a skeptic, you probably noticed that both of the statements were flawed in some way. The first statement suffers from the "duh" factor. If you slept the entire night, you had better report that you felt more rested the next morning! In fact, we should be more concerned that 30 percent of the participants *didn't* feel more rested. But even if the statement compared sleeping on RestWell beds versus the participants' own beds, there would still be a problem. We don't care about how well-rested the participants *feel*, but rather whether how well-rested they actually *are*. So the first statement is providing disingenuous information—it gives us opinions, not facts.

The second statement is also flawed, but slightly less so. Unlike the first statement, the second purports to give us facts. Staying asleep without tossing and turning is a verifiable statement. But the problem is with hidden information. The 70 percent who slept peacefully might sleep just as peacefully in their own beds, and the remaining 30 percent who tossed and turned might be tossers and turners. As such, this statement is also disingenuous.

But what's the point? Information has inherent credibility. If you want to sell a RestWell bed, the best information would be that in a study of people who toss and turn on their own beds, 70 percent slept through the entire night without tossing and turning on a RestWell bed. This statement has internal credibility because it provides the necessary information to make a comparison.

Another way to make information more credible is to ask the jury to challenge it. How? Give the jury verifiable information and ask them to check it out for themselves. You can do this with all sorts of information: the contract clause is ambiguous ("ladies and gentlemen, read it for yourselves and see if you can make heads or tails out of it"), the O.R. nurse lost a sponge ("just look at the post-op checklist and notice what's missing"), or Acme's product infringed on DurCo's product ("look at all the similarities between these two widgets"). This technique is even more effective when you ask the jury to challenge something your opponent says or omits ("listen to their witnesses and see if they can adequately explain why there's no DNA evidence in this case!").

Finally, you can make statements internally credible by appealing to a higher authority. At trial, there are three authorities for the jurors to depend on: the judge, the witnesses, and the lawyers. When we talked about credibility before, we focused on you, the lawyer. The focus here is on the other two—the judge (for legal statements) and your witnesses (for fact and opinion statements). You appeal to the judge's authority when you object, respond to objections, or announce the legal standards. Though that seems obvious, lawyers tend to ignore the effect these things have on the jury. The judge can lend you some of her credibility when your objection is sustained or even when you tell the jury what the charge will say and you turn out to be right.

The same goes for witnesses. The credibility of your witnesses is transferable. For example, when you put a reputed psychiatrist on the stand whose credibility is sparkly clean, the jury will secretly praise *you* for it. But here's the kicker: if that psychiatrist also provides information that is *internally* credible, your own credibility goes through the roof. So when looking for experts, look for three qualities: credentials, communication, and credibility. In other words, look at his resume and interview him in person. Sometimes the case might warrant more (e.g., if there's a lot riding on his testimony or the case is big enough that you can't afford even a minor slip-up). In that event, consider conducting a background check on him, and definitely consult other psychiatrists to verify that his opinions are consistent with the majority opinion in that community.

Your goal, of course, is to get the most credible information before the jury. But what's the connection between credibility and memorability? Think of the last report you read or cited. Or think of the last expert you put on the stand. Chances are you remember who issued the report or where the expert got her Ph.D. more vividly than you remember the content of the report or the testimony. We remember things that impress us. This is obviously no secret, or else the hotshots wouldn't cite the *Harvard* study, or the *CDC* report. But don't overdo it. I've seen many jurors roll their eyes at the twentieth question about the witness's credentials. I've also seen too many lawyers play up this type of institutional credibility, only to watch their witness's personal credibility destroyed on cross.

E. Emotions

Emotions are yet another aspect of stickiness that we've discussed in earlier chapters. But again, the point here is not about persuasion, but rather remembrance. Even so, the same techniques we discussed about pathos and connecting to the jury apply here as well. The authors of *Made to Stick* discuss these emotional connections in two ways—appeals to the audience's self-interest and appeals to their identity. I will discuss how each of these works on juries.

When you think about it, we humans are pretty selfish. We make choices based on what benefits us first and others second. There are some exceptions, such as when we put our children before ourselves. But even in cases involving our families, we see them as extensions of us. In fact, a geneticist will tell you that anything we do for our children is something we are indirectly doing for ourselves, because they are the vessels that carry our genes forward. Pretty heady stuff, but I digress. The point is that some part of us is always looking out for number one.

But on a deeper level, we are social creatures. Many of the decisions we make are based on our positions in our community. The Heath brothers cite a study supporting the position that when we vote, self-interest is not at the top of our list. Rather, "principles—equality, individualism, ideals about government, human rights, and the like—may matter to us even when they violate our immediate self-interest." So we share a sense of responsibility and civic duty that's based in part on our desire for a better world beyond ourselves.

How does this translate into the courtroom? Your presentations will be more sticky if you appeal to one of these human traits. I'll take them in reverse order.

We already appeal to the jurors' sense of civic duty. We thank them for serving, tell them their role, and remind them of their responsibilities to justice. And what we tell them is pretty sincere, because for all the jabs we take at individual jurors, the vast majority of lawyers respect the *institution* of the jury. But as far as stickiness is concerned, you should take this a step further. As the plaintiff, instill in the jury that they are there to right wrongs, to make up for injuries. As the defendant, point out that the jury is there as a check against frivolous lawsuits. As a prosecutor, tell the jury that their purpose is to protect society against criminals. As the defense, remind them that the jury's main function is to protect individuals against arbitrary state action. When you instill a sense of duty in the jurors, chances are that they will pay more attention, and your case will stick.

Personal appeals work slightly differently. At the risk of sounding like a broken record, I'll remind you again that you cannot break the Golden Rule. If you could, the most emotional appeal would obviously be to ask the jurors to put themselves in the position of your client and ask them to decide based on that alone. But since you can't do that, you should resort to the second best thing.

Humanize your client and your witnesses. Give the jury something to *care* about, even if the case is over a contract dispute between two giant corporations. For example, consider the case of *Texaco v. Pennzoil*.[5] How much less personal can a lawsuit get than "tortious interference with a contract"? Nevertheless, Pennzoil's attorneys, including Joe Jamail, who is often referred to as the King of Torts, successfully humanized the case for the jury. Jamail's theme was that this is a case about broken promises, and his evidence was as much about handshakes as it was about signed agreements.

The point is that no matter what type of case you have, there are always people involved. The jurors will remember two people symbolically coming to an agreement with a handshake much better than they will recall the exact date that the documents were executed. If you need more convincing, ask yourself which case sticks out in the jury's mind the most, the one about "broken promises" or the one about "tortious interference with a contract for a stock-purchase merger."

---

5. 729 S.W. 2d 768 (Tex. App—Houston [1st Dist.] 1987).

F. Stories

There are a number of benefits to stories in the trial setting. First of all, we have all been telling stories since we were kids. It is natural to all of us. By starting a presentation with a story you can start on familiar territory in a relaxed and natural manner. How many times have we seen the room shift and the audience lean forward when a speaker begins a story? The reason for this is simple: the speaker has moved from "speechifying" to a more natural means of communication.

It is even better if you can find a real story from your own life. In opening and closing, I often use stories from my own life involving my kids, wife, or other family members. My goal is to tell a story that captures the theme or message in the trial. For example, I tried a case in which we sought to remove a trustee because as he had grown older, his abilities to competently manage the trust and make good decisions for the beneficiaries had greatly diminished. In closing, I told a story about my family's decision to take the keys away from one of my grandparents. My point was that both decisions were difficult and unpleasant, but for the best interest of other drivers, we had to make that difficult decision. I gambled that others on the jury had had a similar experience. In closing, I asked them to do the hard thing and take "the keys" of the trust away from the trustee.

Another story I use in a trial when I want to make the point that a piece of evidence or an argument is beside the point or a distraction comes from my childhood. I tell the story about the day my father and I found an injured bird. When I was about nine, my dad and I were walking though a field and I saw a pretty brown bird that was on the ground and seemed to be hurt. I told my dad that I was going to catch it and take it home, but every time I got close, it moved just out of my reach. Then, after about three near misses and fifteen yards later, it simply flew off. Dad then explained to me that it was a mama quail and it had just distracted me and led me away from its covey where its babies were. I have used that story in closing to say don't let the opposing counsel distract you from what's important. Focus on finding the truth, the covey.

Good storytelling can get you quite a ways to keeping your jury's attention, but it won't always take you the distance. You also have to fight the jury's preconceived notion that you will be boring. It's no secret that trial is tedious. To the juror, trial is no more than an endless procession of witnesses, exhibits, and slides. Nor do the procedural and evidentiary rules we're forced to follow cause or permit much excitement.

So how do you combat this preconception? You have to stand out during your presentation. You don't necessarily have to turn the trial into a TV drama, but you should present your case with an eye toward keeping the jury interested. To do that, you should be the center of attention during trial. As we discussed in Chapter 2, this starts as early as voir dire. When you walk into the courtroom, the jury should immediately recognize that you're going to be a major player in this case. Some lawyers suggest chatting with the court reporter or bailiff before the judge walks in. I agree. Doing this allows you to take control of the courtroom and show the jury that you are in your comfort zone. It also keeps the venire members' attention trained on you.

Another way to keep the jury's attention is to present your case in a style they prefer. As trial lawyers, we cannot ask questions of our potential jurors except in voir dire. So in my voir dire, I always try to ask questions about how people learn. For example, I ask, "If you were going to learn a new subject, would you rather read a book or listen to a lecture?" This demonstrates to the venire panel that you're interested in taking their preferred learning method into consideration in your presentation.

Stickiness is the art of making people remember. Ideas stick in our minds for a number of reasons—they might be poignant, startling, or silly. There's no question that your primary goal at trial should be to persuade. But remember that even the most persuasive arguments mean nothing in the jury room if the jurors don't remember them. If the jury is split on the case, you want the ones who are with you to convince the others. For this to work, your presentation has to be both persuasive *and* sticky. The guidelines you learned in this chapter will help you make those types of presentations, and eventually, lead to better outcomes. In short, SUCCESs will lead to success.

CHAPTER 13

The Jolt Principle: Periodically Jolt Your Jurors so They Do Not Bolt

> "Creative people must entertain lots of silly ideas in order to receive the occasional strokes of genius."
> —*Marshall Cook, actor, director, artist*

In your opening, closing, and examinations, you should plan a jolt about every seven minutes to keep jurors' attention. The best example of this is in the world of TV news. Jolting is a concept I credit to watching my next-door neighbor, Jeff Brady, who anchored the evening news for Channel 8 here in Dallas.[1] Jeff always had a finite amount of time to tell complex stories, while striving to keep his audiences from changing the channel. This is precisely the theory behind a 30-minute newscast, which actually has about 22 minutes of content after you strip away the commercial breaks. The next time you watch the news, also watch the clock. Each newscast has two seven- or eight-minute modules called "news blocks" followed by a two- to three-minute weather and sports block, ending with a one- to two-minute news summary, maybe a feature story, and then a goodnight.

Jeff could not see and judge the reaction of his audience. Therefore, he employed a modular formula aimed at periodically recapturing or refocusing his invisible audience. In a newscast, the jolt is accomplished by methods of substance and style, that is, what is said and how.

Visually: Jeff would turn to another camera and inform the viewers of what was coming up next.

Vocally: Jeff's tone would change (for example, from a somber tone for a serious story to a brighter tone for a lighter piece).

---

1. Today, Jeff has parlayed his news media experience into a new media advocacy agency called the Brady Media Group, of which he is the CEO. You can read more about his experiences past and present at http://www.bradymediagroup.com/about/.

Verbally: Jeff would tease what was in store next for the viewer. For example, there might be a two-second clip of an excited crowd at a city council meeting. Jeff would say, "We'll see what has these good citizens of Dallas so riled up when we come back."

You should plan ahead, and insert "jolt moments" in your trial. But remain alert to see whether your jury is fading at times other than when your jolts are planned. If so, throw out an instant jolt. You can improvise your jolting techniques, or mix and match those mentioned here. Play with your jolts as you plan and practice your presentations. Vary your movement and tone. Use your words to tease your coming attractions right before a break. Call in reinforcements by introducing a video to impeach a witness or moving to a blown-up demonstrative exhibit. Go for a laugh, if it's appropriate. Then throw the jurors a lifeline and reel them back in to your point.

1. Grab Them at the Start

To capture your audience immediately, picture your jury at the start of the trial. Imagine the group of potential jurors that has come to hear the trial about your client's case; envision them drifting into the jury room one by one, sipping coffee, checking their BlackBerrys or iPhones. Where are their minds? Chances are, not thinking about how you are going to grab their attention at the start of the trial. Chances are they're thinking about urgent messages on their handhelds, the car loan application, the stock exchange, their next appointment, their children, or the fight they just had with their spouse. If you were to launch into your opening at full speed, describing your case, you message would blow right past them because they are still focused on the issues and distractions that they brought with them that morning. Once they surface from wrangling with their own problems, the juror finds himself three minutes into your opening and hopelessly lost.. Don't lose your jury from the start. Instead, start by gathering their attention. When I start an examination or an argument, I usually stand silently (and smilingly), looking at the jury until I see and sense that I have their attention and they have laid down their other distracting thoughts. I then start with a punchy or startling point to further ensure I have their attention right from the start.

In 1855, pioneering German psychologist Hermann Ebbinghaus—most famous for his research on the learning curve—conducted one of the earliest studies on memory, using himself as a subject. He memo-

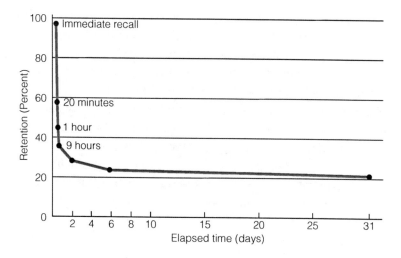

rized lists of nonsense syllables and then tested his memory of the syllables at intervals ranging from 20 minutes to 31 days. Based on this research, he developed what he called the "forgetting curve," which illustrates the exponential nature of forgetting.

As shown in this curve, he found that he remembered less than 40 percent of the items after nine hours, 60 percent by the end of the day, and 90 percent by the end of the week. The basic forgetting rate varies little among individuals, yet one fact remains constant: everyone forgets.

Retention rates can be increased in a number of ways. One is for listeners to actively work on honing their memory skills. But we, as trial lawyers, have no control over whether our jurors are engaged in active mnemonic training, so I will not dwell on that here. What I will point out is that research from Ebbinghaus through today shows that retention rates can be improved by packaging messages so they are:

> ❭ Simpler
> ❭ Catchier
> ❭ More concrete
> ❭ More distinctive
> ❭ More emotionally salient
> ❭ More immediately relevant

Ebbinghaus showed that the forgetting curve is the steepest for nonsensical material; conversely, people better remember vivid or traumatic material.

Another dynamic that Ebbinghaus noted was that the rate of forgetting leveled off over time. A typical graph of the forgetting curve shows that humans tend to halve their memory of newly learned knowledge in a matter of days or weeks unless they consciously review the learned material.[2] Our job as trial lawyers is to review the key themes and facts at regular intervals to prevent the jury from forgetting. Refer back to the chart on p. 147 and you can see how far memory drops off over the course of six days. Most jurors will have lost 80 percent of what they heard in the trial by the sixth day . . . unless you take affirmative steps to help them remember. A few of the things that we have discussed in the book can be used to prevent forgetting. For example, you should keep referring to all of the wonderful demonstratives you have made to support your case. These in essence become flash cards that support your keep arguments and themes. In addition, you can use lead in questions, such as: "Yesterday, we spent some time talking with Mr. Jones about his view of the weather conditions on the day of the accident; I would like to spend the next ten minutes talking with you about yours." With a question like this you have clearly signaled the jury what you would like to talk about and reminded them of Mr. Jones' testimony on the exact subject. There are numerous ways to revisit facts and refresh the jury without asking the same question over and over again. Think about how you can make your point at trial using different methods: questions, demonstratives, demonstrations and the many techniques we have discussed here.

2. Move It!

Have you ever listened to a press conference on the radio? Other than the speaker's voice, the sound you hear is that of cameras snapping loudly whenever the speaker moves. When a speaker raises an arm, cocks his head, claps his hands, or walks away from the podium, he recaptures the audience's attention. Moving naturally, not mechanically, get people's attention.

I have said it before, but let me reiterate the importance of walking away from the podium or from the head of the conference table.

2. http://www.newworldencyclopedia.org/entry/Hermann_Ebbinghaus

When you speak, it feels as if there is an invisible barrier separating you from the audience. You break the barrier by moving away from your expected position. In so doing, you wake up your listeners, connect better, and appear more confident. Try taking a few steps toward the jury when you're giving your opening or delivering your call to action. And when you are making a key point with a witness, move toward him to increase the tension and focus on the exchange between the two of you. A word of caution: You need to be aware of what your judge will allow you to do. And be sure not to get so close to the jury or the witness that they feel threatened by your presence. I encourage a three-point physical presentation model to go along with the message points and proof modules.

> **Position one** is your home base (behind the podium or standing at the head of the table). From this position, you make each of your message points.
> **Position two** is a "step aside." Use it as the position to deliver your anecdotes (step aside for the aside). When you say, "Let me ask you something more about that" in an examination or "Let me tell you a little story" in your closing, step beside the podium, these two actions combined create a mini-interlude in your presentation and it looks as if something just came to you.
> **Position three** is a move to an alternative visual media—a flip chart or a video monitor. When you're using a visual to demonstrate, you can quite naturally move to where the image is generated.

Another method is using volume, which is the art of ups and downs. Dropping your voice to nearly a whisper can be as effective as raising your voice. Lowering your voice tends to get the audience to lean in and listen carefully. I usually start my opening with my volume lower than normal to draw the jury in. When I am using a weapon of discipline to force a witness to tell the truth, the same technique is useful. Both instances are key points in the trial and I want the jury paying close attention.

If you use some of these time-tested methods, your jury will stay alert, anticipating your next move. Jolt them before they have a chance to bolt!

CHAPTER 14

Arming Your Jurors for the "Final Argument"

> "Arguments are often like melodramas—they have
> a predictable beginning, middle, and end."
> —*Gay Hendricks, psychologist, writer and practitioner*
> *in field of personal growth*

There are probably as many styles of closing argument oration as there are attorneys who try cases, from the rhetorical prestidigitation of Johnnie Cochran ("If it doesn't fit, you must acquit") to the bombast of William Jennings Bryan to the understated simplicity of the fictional Atticus Finch. Ultimately, you must choose a style and method that best fit you and will leave you in the best position to achieve your goal: convincing a jury to go your way.

The question that should control the advocate's presentation is "What is the purpose of summation?" One of the best ways to prove your case is to have your friends on the jury do it for you. Jurors have influence on their peers in the jury room, and can exercise tremendous persuasion upon each other. Obviously, this does not happen in a vacuum. You need to have a case that is strong enough to convince at least one juror (in a criminal case) or one to three jurors (in a civil case, depending on the jurisdiction) that your client's position is correct. You'll be better able to convince jurors to argue for your client if there is a bit more margin of error than the bare minimum necessary to hang a jury. Nonetheless, creating and arming your acolytes for the jury deliberations will be necessary in almost any case that is trial-worthy.

What does this have to do with closing arguments? Simple: the closing argument is the time that you teach your favorable jurors how to argue for your result in the jury room.[1] How to do that, and how to build

---
1. *See* 4 HERBERT J. STERN, TRYING CASES TO WIN: SUMMATION 35–36 (1995).

the jurors' trust in you that enables you to persuade them, is the focus of this chapter.

1. What Is the Purpose of the Closing Statement?

After many days or weeks of trial, it's unlikely that jurors are simply wait-ing to hear our closings before making up their minds. The odds are that most of the jurors made up their minds long before closing. Normal decision-making strategies dictate that we begin to lean one way at the outset of trial and continue through trial to look for facts, evidence, and testimony that confirms our leanings. What this means for the advocate is that we cannot hope to have the kind of influence upon jurors at clos-ing that we had at the outset of the trial. There have been many witness examinations and a multitude of exhibits introduced since the opening statements. When an advocate stands to deliver his summation at the end of even a week-long trial, much less a many-week-long trial, he does not face an open-minded group waiting for the final words to make up their minds for them. Of course, people do change their minds and some particularly brilliant closings may achieve that, but grand slams are rare and grand slams in the bottom of the ninth are even rarer.

It is for these reasons that the purpose of closing, particularly after a trial of any length, is to teach your friends on the jury how to argue successfully with your enemies on the same jury. This is because the real "final argument" will not take place in the courtroom, but rather in the adjoining jury room.

The purpose of closing is to teach "your" jurors—that is, the jurors who are on your side—how to argue with and persuade the other jurors in the struggle that lies immediately ahead, so that at the end of the final argument, the ultimate compromises reached—also known as "the ver-dict"—will be closer to your position than your opponent's.

You must pass out weapons to your friends on the jury and demon-strate how to use them to defeat your opponent's best arguments. What are the weapons your allies on the jury will use in their final argument in the jury room? There are several:

> **Trial transcript.** Whenever possible, make extensive use of the trial transcript. Yes, I mean use the actual transcript of testimony. Read it slowly to the jurors so that no one can deny the testimony and all that remains on the other side is whatever can be mustered to ratio-

nalize it away. At the start of the trial, I will ask the court reporter to provide me daily copy. The reporter can usually do this if you ask him ahead of time and are willing to pay a premium for the quick turnaround. Even when there is no daily copy, it is possible to order a page now and then. In cases where funds are limited, purchasing a few dozen pages' worth of transcript can be well worth it.

> **Physical evidence.** I am constantly amazed by advocates who fight like demons to get evidence into the record, only to ignore it in the summation, offering only an elegant oration. Jurors today are visual learners and, to them, seeing is believing. To make them believers, physically handle and display key physical evidence to the jury during summation. And if you are dealing with long documents, show them the exact page you are relying on and give them a page number, especially if your jury is allowed to take notes. In this way, you physically demonstrate to your jurors where to find and how to use the evidence to support their arguments to the other jurors in the jury room.

> **Burden of proof.** By reminding the jurors of the burden borne by your adversary, you provide friendly jurors with additional reasons to dig their heels in when they get in a jury room. Research into juror decision making clearly indicates that the burden of proof is a foreign concept to jurors, and who has to prove what is largely misunderstood.

> **Jury charge.** The one document that most guides the jurors in the jury room is the jury charge. I suggest that you allocate sufficient time in your closing to go through the jury charge and create the decision-making path you want the jurors to employ for each question. Make it simple and clear what you are asking them to do. I either project or blow up the jury charge and literally write in the answer I am asking the jury for in response to each question. If you do not tell them what you want, how are your friendly jurors going to know what to fight for?

2. Persuading the Jury: Closing Statement + Summation = Final Argument

Although we use the phrases "closing," "summation," and "final argument" almost interchangeably, the terms are different. The difference between "summation" and "final argument" is more than semantic. As James McElhaney noted:

> Summation . . . is what must be done when the facts are long and complex, there are many witnesses, or the course of the trial was somehow interrupted. It is a task to undertake when the jury needs help keeping things straight. It is a job most needed when the case has not been well tried. Summing up means going over the evidence. It is not so much argument as it is a preliminary to argument.[2]

Summation is *part* of a final argument, but not the totality of it. Instead, summation is the foundation of the final plea to the jury. To that end, summation of the evidence plus final argument equals the closing.

The key to a persuasive closing is empowering your friendly jurors to persuade their fellow jurors that your client should prevail.[3] If you don't have any by the time of final argument, you probably will not be able to sway any to your side. Why? Prof. McElhaney notes that the jury that "reache[d] a conclusion on its own . . . will hold that conclusion more firmly than if it had merely been told what conclusion to reach."[4]

Obviously, we need to tell the jury what we want from it, but we also want to equip the jury to reach our conclusion on its own. To do this requires tools for the jurors to argue with: highlighting our strong points and the opponent's weak points are obvious methods, but we need these to be connected to something in the juror's mind.

In Texas (unlike many other jurisdictions), we know the Court's Charge to the jury before final argument. Therefore, we have the questions the jury will have to answer, and the Court has charged the jury by the time we make our final argument.

Walking through the Charge step-by-step is required, but a better tactic is to use the Charge in conjunction with daily testimony records to demonstrate both how you want the jury to answer and what the witnesses said that supports that answer. Paraphrasing does not have the same effectiveness as reading the actual testimony from the witness that the court reporter transcribed. Jurors may trust their memories more than yours, but not more than the reporter's transcript; reading the transcript prevents anyone from disputing the accuracy of any "characteriza-

---

2. James W. McElhaney, McElhaney's Trial Notebook 634 (3d ed. 1994).
3. Stern, *supra* note 1, at 31.
4. McElhaney, *supra* note 2, at 646.

tion" of the testimony.[5] Quoting the transcript puts us in good company. Celebrated trial lawyer Edward Bennett Williams quoted extensively from transcripts.[6]

Again, don't lose sight of the powerful effect of physical and demonstrative evidence on your audience, the jury. These are highly effective tools for persuading jurors, too often forgotten in final argument even though we fought tooth and nail to get them admitted. Using physical or demonstrative evidence to support and corroborate the points we make in closing will provide the example that we want our jurors to use to persuade other members of the panel. This tactic is consistent with the overall strategy to enlist our favorable jurors to work for us in the jury room.

Your efforts to deputize your favorable jurors should not include obvious pandering, or any tactic that negatively affects your credibility. You should believe that jurors will see through gimmickry, because they almost certainly will.

In addition, do not assume (or state) that jurors' recollections of the witnesses' testimony will be superior to your own.[7] Nothing is accomplished by this except to strip away some of your own credibility, and such a statement is not true. You have lived with this case (in all likelihood) for months or years and have diligently sorted through the evidence and paid rapt attention to the witnesses; the jurors have not.

Similarly, do not admit your own bias. Every juror knows it is there, but your task is to lead jurors to your client's preferred conclusion by showing that the facts dictate that conclusion. The judge will charge the jury to reach its conclusion without bias or prejudice; therefore, if you admit your own bias the jury will discount what you say.

Also, do not intimate that the jury has superior deductive powers to your own. If that were true, then you would serve no purpose, because a superior result would be obtained if all the evidence was put before a neutral jury to do as it wished without guidance from the attorney.[8] The jury looks to the attorney for guidance and leadership. You as the attorney in charge of the case must provide it.

---

5. Stern, *supra* note 1, at 33.
6. *Id.* at 74–78 (quoting Edward Bennett Williams's closing in Jimmy Hoffa trial); *id.* at 97–99.
7. *See* Robert H. Klonoff & Paul L. Colby, Winning Jury Trials 254–55 (2007).
8. *Id.* at 255–56.

Advice to the contrary abounds, but the summation cannot be prepared pretrial. Once a trial starts, a new life begins. The opposing lawyers exert their influences, witnesses may testify unclearly or differently under the pressure of trial, and the judge may exclude what you once believed was essential evidence. Once the trial is under way, all our pretrial plans, predictions, and stratagems must adapt to the unfolding reality, which is never truly predictable. And that changing reality forces us, the leaders, to at times become followers.

Nothing ever happens exactly as planned, especially in the courtroom. The courtroom contest is as much a place of constant readjustment as any sports field. Only a foolish coach would insist on following a game plan without regard to unfolding events. By the same token, attempting to deliver a summation crafted before trial is as ill-advised as playing the last two minutes of a football game according to a pregame script.

Preparation for summation can begin no earlier than the first witness. If you have a daily transcript, you should be excerpting it every day. During trial, it is wise to get a daily transcript as soon after the end of the day's evidence as possible. You might not read it that night, but in the next few days you or someone from your trial team should review the transcript and identify important testimony to use in closing. Work with your assistant or paralegal to prepare excerpts of the testimony for use in closing. You can set up a three-ring binder in which the excerpts are listed next to their page and line designations. As each witness comes and goes, the binder of important trial testimony grows.

Does this mean that you should deliver the summation as a witness-by-witness recitation of what was said? No. The summation should never be delivered as a witness-by-witness accounting of the trial because the jury will have one of three reactions: (1) we know this; (2) you left out some points the witness said; or (3) when can I get out of here?

3. Structuring the Argument

One of the most important aspects of the closing statement is its structure. When you consider how to structure the argument, keep in mind what your goals are. Obviously, your first goal is to convince the jury that your client should win. But a more subtle goal is to give your advocates persuasive tools for the jury room so that they can convince their skeptical peers to come over to your camp. The structure of your argument should reflect this. It should be easy to follow and emphasize the strengths of your case.

Before we get to the *do*'s, let's talk a major *don't*—don't structure the closing statement in chronological order. Thus far, I've described a trial as a story that you tell in your opening statement and through your witnesses. But the closing statement is the discussion that takes place after everyone has heard the story. When book club members get together to discuss a book, they don't rehash the entire story chapter by chapter. Rather, they talk about the characters, themes, style, and setting. The same goes for you. Don't retell the story—instruct the jury as to what the story *means*.

So what's the best way to structure the argument, if not chronologically? By topic. Your jury is going to retire with a set of instructions that are broken down by topic, so discuss each topic with them one by one. This allows you to relate the facts to the jury in the most persuasive fashion. For example, use the trial excerpts by grouping the testimony in terms of the points or issues at trial. Pull together testimony of disparate witnesses by subject matter. Then when you deliver your summation, the witnesses do not become the organizational structure. Rather, the points can be marshaled in their most persuasive fashion and supported with chapter and verse from different witnesses' testimony.

In your summation, you must instruct the jury to return a verdict in your favor and explain why. This explanation should be limited to no more than three points (e.g., "Acme wins this trial for three reasons. . . ."). Your structural organization will then revolve around these points as they form the foundation and organization of your summation.

Recall from Chapter 12 that your closing statement should be both persuasive and memorable. The points you argue in summation should "stick" in the jurors' minds, so that when they deliberate, their discussion will be framed by *your* theme and the reasons *you* give for returning a favorable verdict. In addition to using the stickiness guidelines in Chapter 12, I also follow two basic principles of memory—primacy and recency. These principles state that people tend to remember the first and last things they hear. Your organization should reflect these principles, too. You should always start and end with the most important points, such as starting with the theme for the case ("This is a case about jealousy and vengeance."). So if you have three points, lead off with the most persuasive point and end with the second strongest, with the weaker one in the middle.

Your closing statement depends on your role as either the plaintiff's or the defendant's attorney. In the vast majority of cases, the plaintiff goes first and last.[9] That is, the plaintiff delivers her closing statement, followed by the defendant's closing statement, and followed finally by the plaintiff's rebuttal. As the plaintiff's attorney, you should simply argue your case and wait to rebut the defendant's case on rebuttal. If you're the defense attorney, however, you need to roll your argument and rebuttal into one. The way to do this is to divide your argument time—present your case first, outlining your theory and detailing the evidence that supports it. Once you have stated your case, move on to attacking your opponent's. Since the plaintiff's argument will be fresh in the jury's mind, you can start with a brief transition into your argument. For example: "The plaintiff just argued that my client broke his promise. I will demonstrate why that argument doesn't hold any water." But even if you decide to begin with this segue, move back into your case before doing any actual rebutting.

As plaintiff's counsel, you need a plan of attack for rebuttal. One mistake I see many attorneys make is to list all the issues raised by the defense counsel, only to address them one by one in rebuttal. Doing this forces you to fight on the defendant's turf, which violates one of the focal lessons in Sun Tzu's famous book *The Art of War*: "Next is the terrain. It can be distant or near. It can be difficult or easy. It can be open or narrow. It also determines your life or death." Never fight the battles where your opponent wants to fight. Fight your battles where you want to fight them.

The easy way around this problem is to outline your rebuttal ahead of time. This is actually easier than it sounds, despite the fact that you don't know what the defense will argue. To fight the battle on your terrain, your rebuttal should be structured much like your initial closing. Before the arguments begin, prepare a very skeletal outline of your clos-

---

9. In a rare few cases, the defendant will be afforded the opportunity to present a surrebuttal argument. But this is always in the trial judge's discretion. *See, e.g., Louisell v. Iowa Dep't of Corr.*, 178 F.3d 1019 (8th Cir. 1999) (holding that trial court's refusal to grant surrebuttal to the defendant was not a due process violation).

ing with lots of space between each line. As the defense delivers its argument attacking your points, locate those points on your outline and write down your opponent's argument. Then either below it or beside it in a second column, write down your response. This way, the outline to your rebuttal will flow just like your closing statement, giving you the opportunity to stress your theme and theory of the case. But you will also be able to rebut each of your opponent's arguments.

No matter which side you're arguing for, you always want to give the jury a road map of your argument. Your argument will be much stickier if it is easy for the jurors to follow. A road map lets the jury know what to expect and prevents them from getting lost in the details. There are a number of ways to do this in your closing statement, but the easiest is to explain how you have organized it: "In the opening, I promised to prove three things. In my closing, I will follow that same structure." It is also important to signal how long you expect to take with your closing. For example, I usually include a time expectation in my substantive outline by telling the jury something like, "I will use our final thirty minutes together going over the testimony and exhibits to demonstrate first how I proved . . . then I will demonstrate how I proved . . . and finally I will demonstrate how I proved. . . ." It is important to tell the jury how long you will be talking so they know what to expect. You do not want to create a distracted jury of clock-watchers constantly wondering how much longer until you are done. An even stronger organizational approach is to literally create a road map. List your proof points on a demonstrative exhibit labeled Plaintiff's Summation that lists your three main points. Remember the Gallup study: we retain better when we both hear and see the message.

Also, give the jury updates as to where you are in your argument. This is generally done through transitions that are extensions of the road map. For example: "And that's why my client wasn't negligent, which was the first point I told you I would prove. Now I'm going to talk about the second point." By using clear transition mechanisms like this, you can signal to the jury where you are on the road map, thereby reinforcing the structure of your argument.

4. Nuts and Bolts of a Closing Statement

This section will cover the content of a closing statement; what do you actually say and do? One solid nuts-and-bolts outline comes from Kenneth Nolan, former editor-in-chief of *Litigation* and a partner at New York's Speiser, Krause, Nolan & Granito.[10] With some adaptations, Nolan's advice is to:

A. Prepare.
B. Practice (verbally, not just mentally).
C. Use simple, active language.
D. Be aggressive and positive.
E. Do not equivocate.
F. Relate the opening to the closing.
G. Be yourself.

These points are fairly self-explanatory, but here are some things to keep in mind:

A. Preparation includes both knowing your case and knowing how you are going to prove it (or disprove the other side's case). Thus, it is crucial to connect what you promised in opening to the evidence admitted at trial and the conclusion to be drawn from it.
B. Practice verbally because you will better discern how things sound if you speak them aloud than if you just silently read the words to yourself. Also, do not merely read a speech. Outline the closing and keep a short outline/list of your key points with you as you deliver the closing. At our firm, we often do this in PowerPoint or similar presentations so that the jury can see the key points as well. Practicing in front of another person also helps, especially if he is not a lawyer (paralegals can be very good for this because they are exemplars of the educated nonlawyers that you want on your jury).
C. Simple, active language is always a problem for attorneys. We have gone through four years of college and three years of law school; we consider ourselves highly educated, and so does the jury. But jurors have common sense and mainstream lifestyles. They speak in plain language that does not require reaching for a dictionary. Thus, in the closing argument the lawyer should speak as a normal person speaks with no legal jargon (other than the key terms from the charge that you want to stick with the jury), no SAT words, and no nonuniversal phrases.[11]

---

10. *See* Kenneth P. Nolan, *Closing Argument, in* 20 LITIG. MANUAL: TRIAL 4, 206–10 (Summer 1994).
11. Nolan gives an example where jurors did not understand the term "red herring" and some wondered what a fish had to do with the case.

D. Strive to make your points, be upbeat and confident, and do not denigrate the other attorney personally. If the opponent's case is extremely weak, based on implausible theories or poor evidence, you should point that out. Discuss the poor evidence, the concessions to weakness the opponent made, and weak links in his evidentiary chain. In a case where the standard of proof is preponderance of the evidence, this means the weak links in the opponent's chain deny him the ability to meet the burden of proof. This is especially true where the opponent relies on an expert's testimony to establish key parts of the case, such as the duty of care or validating a scientific theory.[12]

E. Do not equivocate or understate matters and hope that jurors connect the dots on their own. Instead, the point of closing argument is to lead jurors to the inescapable conclusion that your client should receive a favorable verdict.[13] To do anything less will frustrate the purpose of closing argument, which is to equip the jurors favorable to your case with the ability to persuade their fellows in the jury room.

F. Relating the opening to the closing is warranted when you've complied with the contract you made with the jury in opening your case. If you said in opening that you would show X and you did so in the trial, remind the jury both that you showed X and how you did so. Again, thematic consistency is important. Conversely, if your opponent has failed to deliver on his promises or the opposition's star witnesses did not live up to their hype, the jury will wonder why your opponent failed to meet expectations.[14]

G. None of us can mimic the emotion or rhetoric of other great trial lawyers, nor should we. Do not be fake! If you have real emotion about the case, or real intensity on an issue raised, let the jurors know. If you are capable of rhetorical flourish, indulge yourself. If there are good analogies that cover your situation, by all means, use them. But the jurors have seen you in action for many hours each day for the last few days or weeks; they have a feeling as to who you are and what you are about, and you should reinforce that.

---

12. KLONOFF & COLBY, *supra* note 7, at 268.
13. Stern, *supra* note 1, at 177–81.
14. *See* KLONOFF & COLBY, *supra* note 7, at 265–70, 273–74.

Another nuts-and-bolts list comes from Linda Listrom, a former partner at Chicago's Jenner and Block.[15] Listrom's points are more substantive:

A. Frame the Issues for the Jurors
B. Tie In the Relevant Evidence
C. Tap into Jurors' Experience
D. Show, Don't Tell
E. Use the Jury Instructions
F. Neutralize Bad Facts
G. Resolve Conflicts in the Evidence
H. Fine-Tune the Defense Argument
I. Supply Motives
J. Use Argumentative Exhibits
K. Decide Whether to Argue Damages

Again, this advice is self-explanatory, but here are some suggestions to keep in mind.

A. **Frame the issues.** The facts of the case will not always be in dispute. Sometimes the question will be which facts are more important, or which facts meet the legal burdens. Framing the issues means letting the jurors know which questions are important to answer and which ones are irrelevant.

B. **Argue the evidence.** One curse of closing argument is that there's too much evidence and not enough time to recap all of it. If you don't have enough time to cover all of the evidence in the final argument, use only the evidence that best supports the facts. As you go through your organizational scheme, you should argue how each piece of evidence you introduced supports each of your points.

C. **Use common sense.** Realize that jurors don't come into the courtroom as blank slates. They have real-world experiences that you can play off of. If the case requires jurors to make deductions, use their commonsense experience to help them connect the dots.

D. **Use visuals.** As we learned in previous chapters, people retain information better when it is presented in both verbal and visual form. So when you deliver your closing, show the jury the relevant evidence

---

15. Linda L. Listrom, *Crafting a Closing Argument*, 33 LITIG. MAG. 1 (2007).

as you talk about it. If you're going to discuss physical evidence, hold it in your hands as you talk about it. If you're going to describe a document or a trial transcript, put it on an overhead with relevant information highlighted. One tip is to put a picture of the person who testified next to the transcript to help the jury remember the testimony.

E. **Refer to the jury charge.** Knowing the charge language entails using the key terms in the charge (e.g., "substantial factor," "ordinary person," "reasonable") in your summation to connect your evidence to the standards the jury must use to evaluate it. Conceptually, this is like getting the jury to put mental Post-it notes on key phrases in the charge. By showing them how to fit the evidence within the parameters of the charge questions, you will enable your jurors to lobby for your client.

F. **Defuse the bad facts.** You'll have bad facts in almost every case. After all, if there were no bad facts, your case would probably have settled. Since you know your opponent will hammer away at the facts that are good for her, you need to let the jury know why the bad facts are irrelevant to the issues, or, if they're relevant, why other facts outweigh them. If you ignore the bad facts, you put your credibility at risk.

G. **Resolve evidentiary conflicts.** Sometimes the evidence will point in opposite directions. One witness will say one thing, while another witness will say the opposite. Or one piece of physical evidence will support one version of the facts while another piece will refute that version. Remember, this is precisely why we have juries—to weigh the facts and determine which is more credible. If your case has an evidentiary conflict, your job is to persuade the jury either that the evidence is reconcilable, or that the greater weight of the evidence supports your theory.

H. **Don't ignore motives.** Every trial is rooted in some conflict between people, and people have all sorts of motivations. Sometimes, motive is an element you or your opponent has to prove. But even when it isn't, the jury will have an easier time swallowing your case when you explain to them *why* the actors acted the way they did.

I. **Revisit your demonstratives.** Although the jury may not be able to take the demonstratives back to the jury room with them, you can certainly use them in your closing. If during the case you wrote on a board, drew a chart, or used an overhead, bring back these demonstratives and argue their relevance to the case.

J. **Ask for a verdict.** No matter which side you're on, you need to request that the jury find in your favor. This happens at two levels. At the top level, you obviously want the jury to generally return a verdict in your client's favor. In many jurisdictions, this is enough because the jury charge will simply ask the jury who should win and what damages, if any, should be imposed. Some jurisdictions have more detailed jury instructions, however, that ask the jury to resolve specific factual disputes. This requires a second-level request—you have to let the jury know how you want them to answer each individual question on their charge. You should do this throughout your close, and you can even use it as a transition between topics (e.g., "And that's why you should answer *yes* on question 5.")

K. **Decide whether to argue damages.** If the trial has been bifurcated into two phases (liability and damages), as the plaintiff's lawyer you should always argue for the maximum damages. As the defense lawyer, however, you have something of a dilemma. Some defense lawyers believe that arguing damages is tantamount to admitting liability. But realize that this isn't always the case. Don't put it past the jury to understand alternative arguments (e.g., "My client is not liable, but even if he were, the plaintiff is asking for too much money"). Even if there is a risk that a damages argument is an admission of liability, it's often a risk worth taking.

5. Burden of Proof

Among the most important issues to address in the closing is the burden of proof. Burden of proof in criminal cases is well-known to most jurors; civil burdens of proof are more esoteric. For criminal defendants and civil defendants, the burden of proof is a weapon that your jurors need to use so that they will dig in and refuse to render a verdict for the other side.[16] For instance, if certain evidence is very favorable for you in defense, the logical question for you to have your jurors ask a juror favoring the other side is: "Ask your fellow juror, how can the plaintiff meet his

---

16. Stern, *supra* note 1, at 36–37.

burden when plaintiff clearly said X and plaintiff's own Exhibit 5 clearly shows Y."[17] For prosecutors, the weakest link in the burden of proof is the "reasonableness" of the juror's doubt.

The beyond-reasonable-doubt standard is a shield for criminal defendants, and among the most common explanations of the standard made by a defense attorney to a jury is that he does not have to prove anything—the prosecution must prove its case so that the jury has no reasonable doubt of guilt. The amount of doubt that is reasonable varies; thus the defense attorney will try to minimize the doubt to some minor thing that could be reasonable, and the prosecution will take the opposite tack. The key for a defense attorney is to tell the jury that its doubt as to anything that doesn't add up in the prosecution's case is reasonable, and therefore should result in an acquittal.

Attorneys for plaintiffs use a variety of descriptions. One notable analogy is the scale. Whichever side's evidence weighs just slightly more will tip the case in its favor. One plaintiff's attorney has used this concept with great effect. This lawyer's concept essentially says that the parties are even and all the plaintiff has to do is tilt the scale slightly in its favor to show preponderance of the evidence. Defense attorneys are then left scrambling to point out that to get to the 51 percent proof that equals preponderance of the evidence, the plaintiff still has to build up the first 50 percent, etc. However, it is interesting to note that we as decision makers don't typically decide by the greater weight of the evidence. And, furthermore, when you ask jurors to quantify a "preponderance" of the evidence, you typically get numbers between 80 and 100 percent of the evidence. This is good news or bad depending upon which side of the bar you are on.

From a defense standpoint, pointing out that you don't have to prove anything because you don't have the burden of proof is an effective way to use this concept against your adversary. In addition, the connect-the-dots analogy works for both sides—the plaintiff needs to connect its injury, damages, and causation together, and if the plaintiff fails to do so, the defense must win.

Clear and convincing evidence is another notion altogether. Plaintiffs want to show that this standard is merely a bit stronger than preponderance of the evidence, so they can emphasize that you can have

---

17. *Id.* at 37.

a "firm belief" in something while still having a "reasonable doubt." Defendants would seek to turn that analogy on its head by having jurors raise questions as to the strength of that firm belief.

6. Circumstantial Evidence

Circumstantial evidence is another issue that jurors will get tripped by. If you are the plaintiff or prosecutor and circumstantial evidence is a large part of the case, then you will appreciate this excellent analogy from Craig Spangenberg:

> Remember when Robinson Crusoe was on the island for such a long time all alone? One morning he went down to the beach and there was a footprint on the sand. Knowing that someone else was on the island, he was so overcome with emotion, he fainted.
>
> And why did he faint? Did he see a man? He woke to find Friday standing beside him . . . but he [hadn't] see[n] Friday. Did he see a foot? No. He saw a footprint. That is, he saw marks in the sand, the kind of marks that are made by the human foot. He saw circumstantial evidence. But it was true, it was valid, it was compelling, as it would be to all of you. We live with it all of our lives. So let's look at the facts of this case, for those tracks that prove the truth.[18]

Simply said, "circumstantial evidence" is a dismissive catchphrase for the defense ("it's all just circumstantial evidence"), but circumstantial evidence makes intuitive sense to jurors. Any juror with children does not need to see the kids eating cookies to know why there aren't any left in the cookie jar. That same principle applies in court.

7. Ethics and Objections

The rules of ethics, evidence, and procedure combine to place a number of very real, though definitely manageable, limits on what can be said in final argument. Following are a few thoughts on this important aspect of ensuring a verdict in favor of your client.

> ❯   Statements of personal belief: It is impermissible and unethical for an attorney to "assert personal knowledge of facts in issue or state

---

18. Craig Spangenberg, *Basic Values and the Techniques of Persuasion*, LITIGATION, Summer 1977, at 16.

a personal opinion as to the justness of a cause, the credibility of a witness, the culpability of a civil litigant or the guilt or innocence of the accused."[19]

> Appeals to prejudice or bigotry: It is unethical to attempt to persuade a jury through appeals to racial, religious, ethnic, gender, or other forms of prejudice.

> Misstating the evidence: While it is permissible to draw inferences and conclusions, it is improper to intentionally misstate or mischaracterize evidence in the course of final argument.

> Misstating the law: Attorneys may use final argument to explain relevant facts, to discuss the jury instructions, and to apply the law to the facts of the case. Counsel may not, however, misstate the law or argue for legal interpretations that are contrary to the court's decisions and instructions.

> Misusing evidence: When evidence has been admitted only for a limited or restricted purpose, it is improper to attempt to use it for any other purpose.

> Appeals to the jurors' personal interests: An appeal to the jurors' personal interest invites the jurors to decide on a basis other than the law and evidence. So, for instance, it is improper for a lawyer to tell the jury that a large verdict will result in higher taxes for them or a rise in their insurance costs.

> Insurance: The fact of insurance or extent of coverage is almost always inadmissible and prejudicial.

Objections during final argument follow the same general pattern as objections during witness examinations. Counsel should stand and state succinctly the ground for the objection. There is usually no need to present arguments unless requested by the court.

The best response to an objection is often no response. An objection disrupts the flow of final argument, and an extended colloquy with the judge will only prolong the interruption. A dignified silence will usually be sufficient to allow the judge to rule, and to impress the jury with the basic rudeness of the interruption. When an objection to final argument is sustained, the judge will usually caution the jury to disregard the

---

19. Model Rules of Prof'l Conduct R. 3.4, DR 106(c)(3), (4) (2009).

offending remarks. If the judge does not give such an instruction on its own motion, objecting counsel should consider asking for one.

8. Delivering the Summation

Once you have your themes selected and your evidence organized, it is time to focus on your delivery. In the next few bullet points, I will give you a few pointers on proper delivery to ensure you hold the jury's attention.

> **Beginning:** By the final argument, it should be unnecessary to reintroduce yourself and your cocounsel. Every summation should begin by thanking the jurors. This has nothing to do with advocacy or sycophantic appeals. They have truly fulfilled an important civic duty, sometimes at great personal cost or inconvenience, and their efforts should be recognized. But it is all too easy to overdo the acknowledgments. A simple thank-you on behalf of yourself and your clients is sufficient. It is a matter of basic courtesy.

> **Standing:** Counsel should maintain a respectful distance of about eight to ten feet from the jurors, standing at the center line of the jury box. The argument should be delivered from this distance with no charging to the rail of the jury box or placing your hand upon the jury rail itself. If possible, try to avoid placing a podium between yourself and your audience, the jury. It creates an unnecessary barrier.

> **Moving:** A certain amount of hand and body movement will enliven your presentation and increase the attentiveness of the jurors. Gestures can be used to emphasize important points or to accent differences between your case and your opposition's. Excessive movement, such as constantly returning to the podium to review your notes, is distracting and will undermine your credibility.

> **Using visuals:** A visual aid, such as a demonstrative exhibit that you build by attaching actual exhibits from the trial, can be extremely valuable during summation. Counsel is generally free to use any exhibit that has been admitted into evidence. Counsel may also create a visual display solely for the purpose of final argument.

> **Scripting:** Do not script your argument. By the end of the case, it is always enough to outline the points to be made and to group photocopies of the testimony and the exhibits to use with each of these points. These become, in effect, a living outline of the summation.

❯   **Memorizing:** It is a mistake to try to memorize your final argument. Memorization will yield an affected presentation and carries an extreme risk that you will forget your place or leave out some crucial part.

9. Conclusion

As I've shown, my approach is to develop a thematic consistency from opening statement through closing such that the opening will tell your jury what to expect, the trial will meet that expectation, and the closing will reinforce your success. Thereafter, the task of closing is to ensure that your jurors will adopt your position and work to persuade their fellows. If you have achieved those things, you have made a successful closing statement.

Throughout the pages of this book, I've provided you with the nuts and bolts and the tools necessary to win over any jury. It's up to you to put the tools in your toolbox and put them to good use.

As I have mentioned throughout the book, our retention rate is unfortunately low. Currently you're concerned about the next big trial, what's for dinner, the NBA scores, and whether your daughter should take dance or art next semester. Like your jurors, your mind is racing in a dozen different directions—and to be honest, I'm surprised you made it to the end of the book. If you have found yourself nodding in agreement as you read this book, I would like to challenge you to utilize this book as I have so many in my personal library, by flagging or marking passages that you find helpful and referring to them as part of your trial preparations. If you do, I firmly believe that you will develop the skills to hold your jury's attention and come out victorious in the real final argument—the one that takes place in the jury room.

Index

accusation, impeachment
    technique and, 87–91
acting. see delivery
adverse statements, by witnesses,
    79–82
Analogies Module, 116–117
Anecdotes Module, 117
appearance, credibility and, 50–58
Apple Inc., 128
Aristotle, 47, 49–50
Art of Rhetoric, The (Aristotle),
    47, 49–50
Ash, Mary Kay, 113
attention-deficit disorder
    (ADD), 31
Attention Economy, The
    (Davenport, Beck), 1–2, 31
attentiveness, of jurors, 1–6, 31,
    138–141

bad facts, 177
Beck, John C., 1–2, 31
bias
  cross-examination to, 92
  voir dire and, 7–11
"blurt-out" answers, by witnesses,
    76–78
boardwork, 132–133
body language
  delivery by lawyers, 69
  Jolt Principle and, 162–163

of jurors, 20
Personal Credibility
  Principle and, 48, 53–54,
  56–57
Brady, Jeff, 159
brain
  Personal Credibility
  Principle, 57
  science of, 5, 27–34
burden of proof, 167,
  178–180

Call-to-Action Module, 117
Carville, James, 149
"case slogans," 32
chalkboards, 134
Chunking. see Segmentation
  Principle
circumstantial evidence, 180
civil cases, maintaining credibility
  through cross-examination
  in, 75
clarity, importance of, 69
Clifford, Robert A., 8–11
Clinton, Bill, 149
closing statement, 21. see also
  final argument
  content of, 173–178
  defined, 167–170
  purpose of, 166–167
Cochran, Johnnie, 33

Coherence Principle, 5–6, 39–40,
        137–145
    "Curse of Knowledge,"
        138–141
    simplicity, 141–143
color, dress and, 53
Colvin, Geoff, 43
"comprehension gap," 46,
    48–49
concreteness, 151–153
confidence
    credibility and, 103–104
    importance of, 62–66
confrontation, choosing
        subject of, 84–87. see also
        cross-examination
connecting, with jurors, 65–66
Context Module, 115–116
credibility. see also Personal
        Credibility Principle
    credibility gap, 45–47
    Stickiness Principle,
        153–155
cross-examination, 73–95
    hitchhiking technique, 93–94
    impeaching technique, 73–93
    limiting technique, 94–95
    "Curse of Knowledge,"
        138–141

damages, arguing, 178
Darrow, Clarence, 107
Davenport, Thomas H., 1–2, 31
Definitive Book of Body Language,
    The (Pease, Pease), 48
delivery, 59–72
    confidence, 62–66

importance of, 59–62
    pathos, 66–72
demographics, of jurors, 15–16
demonstratives, 111, 125–126,
        177–178. see also Multimedia
        Principle
denial, by witnesses, 82–84
depositions, inconsistency in,
        84–91
direct examination
    delivery, 63–64
    maintaining credibility through
        cross-examination vs., 81–82
dress, credibility and, 50–58

eagerness, of jurors, 21
Ebbinghaus, Hermann, 160–162
emotions, 155–156
empathy, 66–72
ethics, final argument and,
        180–182
ethos
    credibility through appearance,
        50–58
    defined, 49–50
evidence
    circumstantial, 180
    final argument and, 167,
        176, 177
    improper evidence volunteered
        by witnesses, 78–79
expert witnesses, 108–109
exposition, 108–112
eye contact
    delivery by lawyers, 69
    by jurors, 20
    Personal Credibility Principle, 48

Facts Module, 116
final argument, 21, 165–183
    burden of proof, 167,
        178–180
    circumstantial evidence, 180
    content of closing statement,
        173–178
    defined, 167–170
    delivering summation,
        182–183
    ethics and objections, 180–182
    purpose of closing statement,
        166–167
    structuring, 170–173
flip charts, 133–134
forepersons, Personal Credibility
        Principle and, 51–52

Generation X, 1, 18
Generation Y, 1, 18
Gladwell, Malcolm, 32, 40
glossophobia, 147
"Golden Rule" argument, 68
Google, 142
graphics. see Multimedia Principle

Handbook of Psychology, The
        (Weiner), 29
Headline Module, 115, 117–122
Heath, Chip, 40, 146, 148–149,
        151–152, 155
Heath, Dan, 40, 146, 148–149,
151–152, 155

hitchhiking technique (cross-
        examination), 93–94
honesty, use of, 71
humor, use of, 70

"ideal lawyer," modeling, 64
impeaching technique
        (cross-examination), 73–93
    adverse statements by witnesses,
        79–82
    attacking witnesses' integrity,
        91–93
    "blurt-out" answers by
        witnesses, 76–78
    choosing subject of
        confrontation, 84–87
    cost of credibility attacks on
        witnesses, 74
    denial by witnesses, 82–84
    improper evidence volunteered
        by witnesses, 78–79
    making accusation, 87–91
    uses of, 74–76

Jamail, Joe, 156
Jobs, Steve, 128
Jolt Principle, 5–6, 41–43, 159–163
"Juror Overload," 28, 55
jurors. see also voir dire
    attentiveness of, 1–6
    bias of, 7–11
    demographics of, 15–16
jury charge, 167, 177
jury consultants, 11

"K.I.S.S." (Keep It Short and
        Simple), 37

Laws of Simplicity, The (Maeda),
        140–145
leadership, in jurors, 22
left hemisphere, of brain, 29–30

"legalese"
  Personal Credibility Principle
    and "comprehension gap,"
    48–49
  problems of, 10
Less Is More. see Coherence
  Principle
limiting technique
  (cross-examination), 94–95
Listrom, Linda, 176
logos
  defined, 49–50
  Signaling Principle, 99–104
looping technique, 14–15

Made to Stick: Why Some Ideas
  Survive and Others Die
  (Heath, Heath), 40, 146,
  148–149, 151–152, 155
Maeda, John, 140–145
Mayer, Richard, 29
McDonald's, 152
McElhaney, James, 168
McGraw-Hill, 38
Mehrabian, Albert, 57
metaphors, use of, 69–70
motion in limine, 46
"multimedia effect," of brain,
  29–30
Multimedia Learning (Mayer), 29
Multimedia Principle, 5–6, 38–39,
  125–136
  clarity of graphics, 132–133
  effectiveness of graphics,
  130–131
  final argument, 176–178, 182
  flip charts, 133–134

limiting use of graphics, 126–130
  overheads/PowerPoint
    presentation, 134–136
  power of graphics, 131–132
multisensory concept
  Multimedia Principle, 38
  Stickiness Principle, 40
My Cousin Vinny, (film), 65,
  146–147

narrative
  developing for presentation,
    104–112
  Stickiness Principle and
    storytelling, 157–158
  story vs. process orientation of
    jurors, 18–19
nervousness
  overcoming, 62–66
  Stickiness Principle, 146–148
Nolan, Kenneth, 174
nonverbal communication. see
  body language
notes, for presentation, 100–101

objections, final argument and,
  180–182
Oklahoma v. Raye Dawn Smith, 10
opening statement, 98–99
organization, of presentation,
  104–112
outline, of presentation, 121–122
overheads, 134–136

pathos
  defined, 49–50
  delivery by lawyers, 66–72

Pease, Allan, 48
Pease, Barbara, 48
perception, credibility and, 46
performance. see delivery
Personal Credibility Principle,
    4–6, 35–36, 45–58
  Aristotle on credibility, 47,
    49–50
  building credibility, 47–49
  confidence and, 103–104
  credibility gap, 45–47
  ethos, 49–58
  maintaining credibility through
    cross-examination, 73–95
Plato, 49
PowerPoint presentation, 128,
    134–136
preparation
  developing presentation, 99–104
  for final argument, 174
  importance of, 60, 64–65
  Jolt Principle, 159–163
presentation. see also delivery
  delivering summation, 182–183
  organization of, 99–104
  Segmentation Principle for,
    113–123
  three-point physical
    presentation model, 162–163
primacy, "jolting" and, 42
Proof Module, 116
proofs, 49–50
public speaking, fear of, 147

recency, "jolting" and, 42
reluctance, of jurors, 21
retention, of information, 160–162

right hemisphere, of brain, 29–30
Road Map. see Signaling Principle
Rule 613(a), impeachment
    technique and, 88
rule of three, 31, 113–117

Segmentation Principle, 4–6,
    37–38, 113–123
  Headline Module, 115, 117–122
  preparing wrap-up, 122–123
  rule of three, 113–117
Seven Principles, 35–43
  Coherence Principle, 5–6,
    39–40, 137–145
  Jolt Principle, 5–6, 41–43,
    159–163
  Multimedia Principle, 5–6,
    38–39, 125–136
  Personal Credibility Principle,
    4–6, 35–36, 45–58
  Segmentation Principle, 4–6,
    37–38, 113–123
  Signaling Principle, 4–6, 36–37,
    97–112
  Stickiness Principle, 5–6, 40–41,
    145–158
showmanship, 61. see also
    delivery
Signaling Principle, 4–6, 36–37,
    97–112
  Giving Pertinent Signals (GPS),
    97–98
  logos, 99–104
  opening statement, 98–99
  organizing presentation,
    104–112
  Stickiness Principle and, 151

signposts
  opening statement and, 98–99
  as sound bites, 117
"silent language." see body
    language
simplicity
  need for, 141–143
  Stickiness Principle, 148–150
Simpson, O. J., 33
sincerity, use of, 71
smiling, 48
social media websites, 68
Social Network, The (film),
    106–107
Socrates, 49
Sophists, 49
Sound Bites Module, 117
Spangenberg, Craig, 180
standing, Personal Credibility
    Principle and, 56–57
Stickiness Principle, 5–6, 40–41,
    145–158
  achieving "SUCCESs," 146,
    148–158
  nervousness, 146–148
stories, 157–158
"SUCCESs," 146, 148–158
  concreteness, 151–153
  credibility, 153–155
  emotions, 155–156
  simplicity, 148–150
  stories, 157–158
  unexpectedness, 150–151
Summary Module, 117
summation. see also final
    argument
  defined, 167–170
  delivering, 182–183

technology
  attentiveness of jurors and,
    1–6
  social media websites used for
    voir dire, 68
Texaco v. Pennzoil, 156
Texas, Court's Charge in, 168
three-point physical presentation
    model, 163
Tillotson, Jeff, 61
Time to Kill, A (film), 66–67
Tipping Point, The (Gladwell),
    32, 40
transitions
  opening statement and, 98–99
  organization of presentation
    and, 108–109
trial transcripts, for closing
    statement, 166–167
tweeting, 2

unexpectedness, 150–151
University of Southern California,
    57

verbal information processing, 29
verdict, asking for, 178
visual information. see also
    Multimedia Principle
  Multimedia Principle, 38
  processing of, 29
voir dire, 7–25
  challenging jurors for cause,
    24–25
  checklist, 16–22
  delivery by lawyers, 67–68
  goals for, 7–11
  process of, 11–16

time-saving techniques for, 22–24

Weiner, Irving, 29
Weiss-McGrath Report
    (McGraw-Hill), 38
whiteboards, 134

Williams, Edward Bennett, 169
witnesses. see cross-examination
wrap-up, for presentation, 122–123